Praise for **TRUTH**

"*Truth Warriors* will give you an enti[...] confidence in your decision-making process. By understanding the contrast of rational and intuitive styles and the need to produce positive tension, we can learn to produce better outcomes. Whether professionally or personally, Christi teaches us to take a leadership role in being bold, transformative and deliberate in our action to ultimately decide on the best path forward." —Lee Ferreira, general manager, Ferring Canada

"Christi Scarrow looks for and fights for truth in all aspects of her life, professionally and personally. Her tenacity and passion make her a warrior in action. Her journey is woven into this book and the book is woven into her journey. I believe that journey will resonate with and enlighten many professionals looking for truth as a compass to live their life by." —Drew Munro, partner, Lighthouse NINE Group

"This is the book I didn't realize I needed. Christi challenges her readers to reflect on how we approach decision making in all aspects of our lives. With personal stories and tangible strategies, Christi carries her audience through a journey of discovering the Truth Warrior in us all, leaving her readers enlightened and wanting more." —Leanne Slaney, social worker, Halton Healthcare

"Christi Scarrow is a gifted writer who makes the experience raw, real and relatable. Whether you like to dive into your favorite book until it's done or pick it up and put it down at your own pace, the journey to becoming your Truth Warrior is as unique and beautiful as this book." —Brea Corbet, president, Change of Heart Fitness

"Reading *Truth Warriors* will make your own life better, and the lives of everyone you interact with better as well. It is a must-read for anyone who cares about bringing out the best in people and in making better decisions." —Phil Drouillard, founder and chair, Lighthouse NINE Group

More Praise for **TRUTH WARRIORS**

"*Truth Warriors* is a personal, practical and potential-releasing guide to finding your voice and making better decisions. It includes straightforward tools supported by impactful examples from the author and those who have helped to light her way. A great read and something you can immediately apply to your life." —Greg Smith, podcast host and author of *In Search of Safe Brave Spaces*

"*Truth Warriors* offers something for every leader. It can be used by a wide range of professionals to reflect on their own beliefs, biases, and decision-making processes. Through the use of personal and work examples, from herself and other leaders in history, Christi Scarrow helps bring truth to life in a way that everyone can relate to." —Jennifer Tunnicliffe, professor of human rights history, Ryerson University

"*Truth Warriors* is packed with fascinating stories, novel insights, and practical tips for every leader who has something worth fighting for." —Liane Davey, *New York Times* bestselling author of *You First* and *The Good Fight*

"Christi Scarrow brings forth an insightful framework to guide today and tomorrow's leaders in the Dance nowadays required to powerfully leverage personal and collective Truths in the delivery of superior results." —Luc Mongeau, president, Weston Foods

TRUTH WARRIORS

The Battle to Hear, Be Heard and Make Decisions that Count

Christi Scarrow

Rock's Mills Press
Oakville, Ontario
2021

Published by
Rock's Mills Press
www.rocksmillspress.com

Front cover design by The Garden North America Inc.
Lightbulb icon: Adapted from an image by Eucalyp at www.flaticon.com.
Author photo by Brea Corbet

For information about this book, including bulk, bookstore, and library orders, email us at customer.service@rocksmillspress.com.

Dedication

To my mother who taught me how to speak up,
to my father who taught me to listen
and to my tribe of Truth Warriors who continue to challenge my beliefs by
sharing their truth.
Thank you for being part of my battle.

Additional Resources

Throughout this book you will see this icon in the margins of certain pages. It indicates that additional resources are available to you: videos, downloadable tools or links to other useful content. You can find all these resources at:

www.truthwarriors.ca/resources

Contents

Introduction 1

Part One: Becoming the Truth Warrior 5
1. What is Truth? 5
2. Who is the Warrior? 9
3. Why We Need to Make Decisions that Count 15
4. Why We Believe 25
5. The Dance of the Truth Warrior 37

Part Two: Seek Truth: Balancing Rational and Intuitive... 41
6. Finding the Balance 43
7. The Rational Truth Seeker 45
8. Why We Need Less Information 49
9. The Intuitive Truth Seeker 53
10. Why We Need More Information 57
11. The Dance of Seeking Truth 61

Part Three: Speak Truth: Leaning In and Out of Conflict .. 67
12. The Conflict Aggressive 69
13. Why We Need Less Conflict 71
14. The Conflict Avoidant 77
15. Why We Need More Conflict 79
16. The Dance of Speaking Truth 91

Part Four: The Warrior Within Us **93**

17. Understanding Your Decision and Conflict Style ... 95
18. The Pensive Scientist 99
19. The Fact Evangelist 103
20. The Idea Holder 109
21. The Passion Proclaimer 113
22. Moving Within Truth 119

Part Five: Lead Truth: Building Your Battle Cry **123**

23. The Battle Before You 125
24. Let Go and Build Up 127
25. Create Harmony and Tension 141
26. Be Humble and Bold 157

Conclusion 171
Additional Resources 173
Acknowledgements 175
About the Author 177

TRUTH WARRIORS

Introduction

You are on a journey. You are finding your truth. You may already be discovering that it is not yours alone. Your truth is biased by perception and shaped by your experience. It defines your beliefs. The world may feel broken, or it may feel limitless. You wonder what your future holds. You want your life to have purpose and your work to add value. You need to make the best decisions you can, in uncertain times. You want to make a better world. It is in your hands to create.

You are ambitious but understand the need for balance. You know you need collaboration to be successful but you are not quite sure how to get it right. Decisions are becoming more complex and you are sometimes uncertain about the best way to make them. You are being pushed to decide without all the information, and pushing others to do the same. You may go with your gut or stick to logic. Your goal is to make effective but timely decisions. You need to figure out when to let go of your truth and how to build up systems to enable the truths of others.

You are a leader. You may be leading a team or driving change in the world. You might wonder if your expectations are too high, or too low. You recognize that people have different needs but are not sure how to meet them all. You are trying to balance urgency with accuracy. You are trying to be respectful but also challenge the status quo. You need to create both harmony and tension.

You have ideas that can drive change. You are sometimes a lone voice in a sea of bureaucracy or a lost soul filled with self-doubt. You want those above you to hear your voice. You strive to make things better. You are afraid to make mistakes, but you do. You respect others and want to be respected for the value you offer. You need to know when to be bold and when to stay humble.

This is the dance of the Truth Warrior—to seek, speak and lead truth. Truth Warriors know when to stand strong and when to bend. They know when to trust their experience or seek more information. They know when to dance or stay still. Great leaders understand they are on a journey, one that will never be perfect. They know that the best decisions are made with diverse perspectives, harmony and positive tension. The Truth Warrior recognizes the common desire for peace can only be achieved through battle—positive, respectful, change-educing battle.

This book is about the battles that came before you. My hope is to help you learn from my mistakes and the mistakes and triumphs of great leaders who have shared their stories with me. The pages you are about to read are filled with practical tips to help you make better decisions in your job and in your life. My goal is to allow you to fail, as I have failed, but inspire you to think a little differently. I will share a model that brings together decision and conflict styles that will help you understand your natural tendencies. This is the start to becoming a Truth Warrior.

We are all in this battle together. We all have an opportunity to make decisions that count. To do so we must look for facts but trust our experience, believe in ourselves and yet question our own truth. We must be willing to speak up but also to be quiet. Making better decisions is about making your voice about *our* voice and your truth about *our* truth. Only then can we change the world.

PART ONE

Becoming the TRUTH WARRIOR

1. What is Truth?

Three baseball umpires are discussing how they decide what's a ball and what's a strike. The first says, "There are balls and there are strikes; I call them as they are." The second says, "There are balls and there are strikes; I call them as I see them." The third says, "There are balls and there are strikes and they ain't nothin' till I call them."

Truth exists in our perception of reality. The definition of truth is not static nor easily agreed upon. The answer to the question "What is truth?" has been debated for thousands of years. I would be naïve to think I can answer that question here. The current edition of the Merriam-Webster dictionary defines truth as "the body of real things, events and facts" but also as "a transcendent fundamental or spiritual reality." Both descriptions imply the existence of an underlying reality which itself is defined as "the state of things as they actually exist, as opposed to an idealistic or notional idea of them." But *how* do "they" exist? They exist within our collective experience.

The same dictionary also describes truth as "sincerity in action, character and utterance." So if I believe something and express that belief honestly, does that make it true? Is it possible that both you and I can be right at the same time? When someone says "the truth" they are talking about their own subjective experiences and observations that they've made based on those experiences. And if truth is what we believe, is it possible that we can lie even to ourselves?

"We believe what we tell ourselves, so let's make sure we tell ourselves the truth." —Sophie Grégoire Trudeau

My 11-year-old son once told me that he was worthless. It is a lie he tells himself regularly. When his anxiety gets the better of him, his truth is one where he believes the worst about himself. He believes he has no friends, even though I see him playing with them at school. He believes he is not smart, even though he gets great marks in school. He believes he is not good at sports, even though he was one of the top goal scorers on his hockey team. His truth does not consider the reality of the facts. I believe we must pause to confirm if our "truth" is really "true" or if our inner voice is leading us down the wrong path. We must recognize that truth is personal and fluid.

Truth is personal.

Two men enter a courtroom. One has a bandage on his face that clearly indicates a broken nose. He is accusing the other man of breaking his nose during a fight a few weeks ago. The defendant recounts his version of the events, claiming that the victim started an argument with him and then physically attacked him. The defendant claims he acted in self-defence, shoving the other man. The attacker fell over backwards; his legs swung up and hit him in his face, breaking his nose.

The victim describes it differently. He agrees that he started the argument, claiming that the defendant was being rude to the wait staff. He repeatedly asked the man to stop and when he did not, moved towards him. The defendant then swung at him, hitting him in the nose and causing him to fall over backwards.

Which one is telling the truth? Both believe their version of the story to be accurate. Neither is lying about what they experienced. Both perspectives are plausible and both men believe that their perspective is correct.

There is an ancient parable of "the blind men and the elephant" that teaches of the importance of perspective and truth. Each blind man is touching a different part of the elephant and has to guess what they are examining. The man touching the tusk believes it is a spear. The man next to the elephant's leg believes it to be a tree. The man at the tail believes it is a snake and the man resting against the elephant's side believes it to be a wall. Each can only make a guess based on their own perspective. But the truth is: *It is an elephant.*

This elephant represents our collective truth. The individual interpretations are our personal truths. Truth Warriors have the courage to bring their personal truth to the group and are curious enough to listen to the truths of others.

Those who believe truth is absolute will tell you that there can only be one version of an event. There are those who believe in Aristotle's law of non-contradiction, which states that two contradictory propositions cannot both be true in the same sense at the same time. Either God exists or he doesn't. Either a car is blue or it isn't. There can be no in-between. But in fact, we have seen an in-between.

In February 2015, an image of a dress circulated on the internet that threw a wrench into the concept of the law of non-contradiction. People were asked to describe the dress's colour. Some claimed it was blue and black while others said it was white and gold. It could not be both. But it was. People described it as either/or. Their individual perceptions of colour changed their description of the dress. We can view the exact same thing and yet each perceive it differently.

Our truth is personal and the broader truth is a collection of those perceptions. Truth Warriors acknowledge this fact when they realize that their truth is not **THE** truth and instead recognize the existence of the "in-between." They also need to acknowledge that the truth of today will not be the truth of tomorrow. Truth moves with our collective experience. Truth is fluid.

Truth is fluid. On the morning of Thursday, December 12, 1799, George Washington developed a fever and was struggling to breathe. Throughout the day, his condition continued to deteriorate, causing him to seek treatment from three different doctors. They tried various treatments. One of the primary ones was bloodletting. Two days after falling ill, on December 14, 1799, George Washington passed away. In the course of his treatment, the doctors bled him four times and extracted a total of thirty-two ounces of blood. Many believe this treatment was the primary cause of his death.

At the time of Washington's death, bloodletting was a common and widely accepted medical practice. It remained so until late in the 19th century. Today we treat cancer with chemotherapy and radiation. Is it possible that this treatment protocol will someday seem equally archaic? Cancer was once thought to be completely incurable. Ancient physicians recognized that even when a cancerous tumour was surgically removed, it would grow back. They saw no possible treatment once a cancer had spread and were concerned about the fatal implications of any efforts at treatment.

If we believe today that the best treatment for cancer is chemotherapy, could that belief not change in the future? If we didn't believe that things could be different, then we wouldn't be looking for new treatments. What if someone discovers the cure but nobody believes them because they are so set in the belief that chemo is the best option? What if they believe that the scientist who finds the cure is only doing it to make money and therefore don't trust them?

Truth is a dance. If sustainable by other facts, it can change what we observe to be "facts." In his book *The Relativity of Wrong*, Isaac Asimov talks about this concept more in detail. He suggests that scientific theories are never right or wrong; rather, theories gradually are improved in such a way that new theories are a little less wrong than earlier ones. The lesson for me in this is that we must never consider ourselves to be fully right. We can only be less wrong than before. We can never be confident in the truth of today.

Truth is fluid and shifts with time and experience. Truth Warriors allow themselves to seek new information and strive to be less wrong than before. Truth is a dance. It is a series of movements that shift over time. The dancers have a role to play. They can move together or apart, quickly or slowly. They can be centre-stage or in the background. Each dancer's perspective on the dance and their role in it is different. Truth, like a dance, is both personal and fluid. It represents the collection of our beliefs over a period of time. It *moves* with us. This is the dance we must all do. It is the dance of the Warrior.

2. Who is the Warrior?

The Warrior speaks up for what is right. In late 2019, Brett Crozier was assigned command of the nuclear aircraft carrier *USS Theodore Roosevelt*. He was a heavily experienced decorated naval officer. The ship was deployed to the Pacific on March 24, 2020, with 4,965 seamen aboard. Only a few days after deployment, dozens of soldiers tested positive for COVID-19. When the ship docked in Guam on March 27, it offloaded approximately 100 soldiers and Crozier asked to have most of the rest of the crew taken ashore, expressing concern about being able to contain the virus in the close quarters of the ship. His superiors denied him that request. On March 30, Crozier emailed a four-page memo to ten navy officers in his chain of command requesting the crew be evacuated and quarantined ashore. The email was leaked and published in the *San Francisco Chronicle* and subsequently went viral. On April 1, the carrier was evacuated and one day later, the U.S. Navy relieved Crozier of his duties. At that time 114 of his crew members had tested positive, including Crozier himself. After subsequent testing, 660 soldiers in total tested positive, some with no symptoms but capable of transmitting the virus.

Brett Crozier spoke the truth, even though it resulted in his dismissal. It is possible that he anticipated that his letter might get leaked. As his superior argued in a later interview, sending such a memo "represented just extremely poor judgment, because once you do that in this digital era, you know that there is no way that you can control where that information's going to go."

Crozier was courageous and he embraced conflict. He paid a personal price but he also achieved a substantial victory. His crew sent him off amidst cheers and public support was overwhelmingly positive. He may have saved lives by expressing his opinion. He was a Warrior.

Meriam Webster describes a Warrior as "a person engaged in some struggle or conflict." A Warrior's job is not just to fight. It is to stand up for what is right and to back down when wrong. The challenge is recognizing the difference. The Warrior must speak up but also must listen to the truth of others.

The Warrior listens to the truths of others.

In 2019, I attended a sales conference that featured two amazing woman leaders. One of them was 15 and the other was 18. I was initially inspired by their bravery, their ability to stand on a stage in front of hundreds of people, many of them twice their age. They were asking us to listen. To listen to the challenges faced by their generation and more importantly their desires. They were representing a company they had founded called ThinkGenZ. The goal of that organization was to listen to others. To collectively gather and share the insights of their generation with brands that did not understand them. They also understood the importance of showcasing how their generation could change the world. Their website highlights young thought leaders like themselves—teens fighting for social change.

Ella Verhoeven, one of the founding members, wrote a blog post entitled " 'OK, Boomer'—Generational Shaming Isn't the Solution." At 18 years of age, she already understands that belonging to different generations shouldn't divide us. In her blog, she states, "Sadly, generational labeling and name-calling isn't going to change our reality. We need to engage in conversations that will inspire entirely new ways of solving global problems, TOGETHER." Both Ella and her sister are Warriors. They are listening to the voices of others. They are encouraging us to do the same.

"Leaders who don't listen will eventually be surrounded by people who have nothing to say." —Andy Stanley

Our ability to make better decisions depends on our ability to make educated choices and to understand other alternatives. If we avoid conflict and are unwilling to share our thoughts, we are withholding valuable information. If we are overbearing with our own perspectives and are conflict-aggressive, then we are missing the information of others. When we don't have all the information, we make worse decisions.

Conflict as a part of decision-making does not mean competing with one another. Too often, team decision-making pits one idea against another with each person trying to persuade the leader why their idea is best. This is not my intent. Instead, my suggestion is one of brave but respectful conflict. The concept of leaning in and out of conflict means that you balance the voices of everyone. It is a commitment to "hold space" and actively support healthy dialogue. You consider the perspectives of others but also are willing to speak your voice.

Warriors know that listening to others is just as important as speaking their truth. They recognize that alternative perspectives are necessary for better decisions. Conflict does not mean that we compete for truth, but instead work towards it together. Like truth, conflict is a spectrum. At times we must lean into it. At times we must lean out. The Warrior dances within conflict.

> **The Warrior dances within conflict.**

In her TED talk, "Why you think you are right even when you are wrong," Julia Galef shares two mindsets that are key to the Warrior mindset: the Soldier and the Scout.

She describes the Scout's job in battle as one of understanding: "The scout is the one going out, mapping the terrain, identifying potential obstacles. And the scout may hope to learn that, say, there's a bridge in a convenient location across a river. But above all, the scout wants to know what's really there, as accurately as possible."

Conversely, the soldier is driven to a goal. In describing this role, Julia says: "Your adrenaline is elevated, and your actions are stemming from these deeply ingrained reflexes, reflexes rooted in a need to protect yourself and your side and to defeat the enemy."

Each plays a role in how we make better decisions. The Warrior needs to both understand and act—to seek and speak truth. The Warrior must recognize the balance required to achieve both of these. They must understand that the battle for peace can only be achieved through conflict.

As our world becomes more divided, people tend to take increasingly extreme positions on the conflict spectrum. Those who are insistent on the rightness of their beliefs and unwilling to consider the beliefs of others dig their heels in and fight harder. Those who feel unheard or who fear conflict, draw back into themselves. They surround themselves with those who believe the same things because that is the safe place to be.

It is the flight or fight response. If we are conflict-aggressive, we fight. If we are conflict-avoidant we flee. Neither approach allows us to resolve the conflict.

"Sometimes what gets in the way, is the way." —Brené Brown

The word conflict has negative connotations. A thesaurus will tell you that synonyms include *battle*, *clash*, and *combat*. This is not my version of conflict. The Warrior embraces conflict in a different way. Another synonym for conflict is the word *engagement*. This better describes my perception. Embracing conflict has to do with a willingness to express your truth. It does not mean that you don't listen to the truths of others, but that instead you are willing to share your truth.

Conflict encompasses two behavioural extremes: those who are conflict-aggressive and those who are conflict-avoidant. Conflict-aggressors come across as confident in their opinions. They tend to be good influencers. They don't like to let issues fester. They are more willing to express their opinion of or discontent with a situation or with others. There is also a risk to this style. The directness of these individuals can be off-putting and can sometimes get in the way of their actual message. If too confrontational, this style can damage relationships. If the conflict is based on a strong opinion, this individual may miss useful contributions from others. Leaders in this bucket may erode trust with their team.

Conflict-avoidant individuals have harmonious relationships. People feel heard by them and are comfortable around them because they know they will not be confronted. They are great peacekeepers. The risk for these individuals involves both themselves and the groups they support. Resentment may build up easily when group members feel unheard or misunderstood and issues are unresolved. Some people may even come to think that others are aware of problems and purposely not addressing the issue when this may not in fact be the case. Leaders who fall into this bucket may not be addressing performance issues.

On either end of the conflict spectrum, we make poor decisions. Just like our decision styles, conflict is a dance we must do. Although most of us dislike conflict, some of us are better at speaking our truth. Others need to find their voice. When we navigate complex decisions, we need to be able to move between the extremes of conflict. We must be *conflict-responsible*. We need to know when to speak and when to listen. Only then can we make better decisions.

3. Why We Need to Make Decisions that Count

We need to make decisions that count for OURSELVES.

My father used to say, "I'd rather die young with a cigarette in my mouth than quit smoking." He was diagnosed with lung cancer at the age of 67. On August 30, the day he was told of this diagnosis, he smoked his last cigarette. On December 6 of that same year, he died.

In the months between his diagnosis and his death, he had much to think about. What I saw in his eyes and heard in his words was regret. Regret that the choices he made had possibly led to this result. In the moment, as he lived his life, it felt like the right philosophy: get the most out of life. But ultimately this philosophy had long-term consequences that were not completely unpredictable. As humans, we are the only species that is aware of our own mortality—we will all die—but not one of us actually believes it. Those who choose to smoke know the risk, but do not ultimately envision a long-term result. The choices we make every day oftentimes ignore these same factors. We are all prone to making short-term decisions without considering their long-term implications.

I have never been a smoker and therefore cannot claim to understand his addiction. My mother, once a smoker herself, tried to help me understand it by telling me to "imagine being told that you can no longer drink water. That's what it feels like to quit smoking." A thirst that could never be quenched. My dad was held tight by this addiction. It was so great that for him considering the alternative was nearly impossible.

My father made bad decisions. The first and most obvious was continuing to smoke. What frustrated me most was his inability to try to quit. Although I knew it couldn't be easy for him, I wanted to see him make the effort. Instead, he dabbled. He reduced the amount he smoked but never stopped completely for more than a week. Until he was diagnosed. That day he smoked his last cigarette. In the end, the choice was obvious. He wanted to live. He wanted to breathe. Once he did stop, he acknowledged how much easier it had been than he thought it would be. The anticipation of never smoking another cigarette was in fact worse than the actual impact of fighting the physical and psychological addition. This realization only deepened his regret.

My dad made another unfortunate choice in this journey. His battle with cancer actually started much earlier than I knew. He had been diagnosed with COPD and was being regularly checked for any signs of cancer. A scan that had taken place four years earlier found a concerning lesion. He never followed up. When his cancer was officially diagnosed, it was already Stage 4. The chance of surviving more than five years was only 4.7 percent. My father allowed his fear to get in the way of considering the unfathomable. He knew his risk of cancer was high. His desire for smoking was even higher and his fear of hearing what he didn't want to hear stopped him. He stopped himself from pursuing the truth until it was too late to do anything about it.

I don't blame my father for the choices he made. No one starts smoking with the belief that it will result in their death. We all have our addictions and vices that become almost impossible to stop. We make decisions every day, some simple, some complex. We decide what to have for dinner, or what job to take, or the best way to care for our children. Each is an opportunity to think differently. Each may have ramifications that are worth considering.

I am not immune to poor decisions. I don't exercise enough or eat right. I allow my kids too much screen time. I spend too much time online as well. Every day is about a choice. Our goal as Truth Warriors is to consider the implications of these decisions before it is too late. We must avoid regret but also recognize that we will make bad decisions. Many are rectifiable. Failure is essential for learning.

Only by starting with our own individual decision-making can we move on to support those around us. Our teams—our tribes—need a leader to help us make the right decisions for the business.

We need to make decisions that count for our TRIBE.

In 2000, John Antioco was the CEO of Blockbuster, which at that time was the leader in home movie distribution with thousands of retail locations and millions of customers. A man by the name of Reed Hastings came to Antioco's office to pitch an idea. He proposed that offering subscriptions rather than rentals would be more customer friendly, and would remove the pain point of late fees. He asked that Blockbuster consider supporting his subscription service online and promote access to it within their stores. That service was Netflix.

Anitoco and his team rejected the idea. As we all know, the result of this decision was catastrophic. Blockbuster went bankrupt in 2010 and today Netflix is the leading streaming service.

Anitoco was a good leader. He had doubled the revenues of Blockbuster during his time in the business. But several decisions he made during his tenure resulted in his release from the business and the ultimate demise of Blockbuster. The first of these decisions involved the model itself. A large portion of Blockbuster's revenue was derived from customer late fees. Success depended on penalizing their customers rather than removing their pain points. The Netflix model removed this source of revenue. Anitoco and his team did not know how to adequately address this revenue gap without putting their profitability at risk.

As Netflix and other streaming services started to take hold, Anitoco began to recognize the threat they posed to his business. He responded by removing late fees and launching Blockbuster online. This substantially reduced the company's profitability. As shareholders felt the pain of these shifts, they also questioned his leadership. Carl Icahn was an activist investor who pushed to removing Anitoco as CEO. Anitoco lost the support of the board and was let go in 2005.

In an article he wrote for the *Harvard Business Review* in June 2011, Antioco himself stated, "I didn't believe that technology would threaten Blockbuster as fast as critics thought." He added: "Having contentious directors was a nightmare; as management, we spent much of our time justifying everything we did." John Antioco made two mistakes that ultimately led to the demise of Blockbuster. He didn't take enough time to consider the alternatives to his existing model, and he failed to gain support for the change he was trying to create within his organization.

Good decision making is essential to organizational success. Leaders need to chart the path, to make decisions about the direction the company is going and the capabilities, behaviours and processes required to get there. They need to decide who is responsible for what and what to do when results are not as expected. They need to build and support a tribe that makes better decisions.

If Anitoco could replay the tape on his career, he might have established a team, his tribe of Truth Warriors to help both support and challenge his vision. A tribe of Truth Warriors has diverse perspectives. Leaders support their tribe by role-modelling a balance of risk taking and thoughtful consideration in decision-making. They are systematic in validating their beliefs. They reward risk-taking and mistakes and encourage team members to challenge one another. If we build a tribe of Truth Warriors, we can work collaboratively towards better business decisions. If we build better tribes, we can create an army.

We need to make decisions that count for our ARMY.

Buffy Summers, although a fictional character, is one of my favourite Truth Warriors. If you don't know who she is, I suggest you check her out. She is Buffy the Vampire Slayer, a teenage girl chosen as the only person on earth with the strength and duty to fight vampires. Although many slayers have come before her, she is unique in her approach. What gives her strength is the people she surrounds herself with. It is her tribe.

Buffy fights both figurative and real demons. She rarely does it alone. When the TV series first began, we were introduced to her high-school friends. None of them are blessed with the same skill Buffy has, but they become pivotal in her survival. At various points in the series, each has a role to play in saving the world. Each also plays a role in putting the world at risk.

In the last season, Buffy must fight one of the strongest demons in history. He is described as the vampire that vampires fear. By this point, her high-school friends have become powerful allies with skills of their own. Buffy begins recruiting women across the world to help her cause. These women have no obvious powers and are afraid to fight. In the episode "Bring on the Night" Buffy's watcher Gilles informs her that there is a plan to kill all these women and anything associated with the Slayer. During this episode, one of the new recruits flees in fear and is killed by this vampire. Buffy tries to save her and battles the monster. She returns home exhausted. After resting, she comes downstairs to overhear her friends expressing their concern about her condition and ability to fight this battle. Her response to them is very powerful:

> You're right. We don't know how to fight it. We don't know when it will come. We can't run. We can't hide.... I am beyond tired and I am beyond scared. I'm standing on the mouth of hell and it is going swallow me whole. And it'll choke on me.... We're not ready? *They're* not ready. They think we're going wait for the end to come, like we always do. I'm done waiting. They want an apocalypse? Well, we'll give 'em one. Anyone else who wants to run, do it now, 'cause we just became an army. We just declared war. From now on we won't just face our worst fears, we will seek them out.... There is only one thing on this earth more powerful than evil. And that's us.

She rallies her tribe and creates an army. She prepares them for the battle, both physically and mentally. She believes in them and she creates a culture of strength. At the end of the series, Buffy makes a bold choice in humility. The premise of the entire show is based on her being the "chosen one." That she alone must fight the demons. Each episode begins with the words, "In every generation, one Slayer is born." In the last episode of the series, Buffy gives up her role as the Slayer, instead imparting her powers on the army she has created and girls across the world:

So I say we change the rule. I say my power should be our power. From now on, every girl in the world who might be a slayer, will be a slayer. Every girl who could have the power, will have the power. Can stand up and will stand up. Slayers, every one of us.

Buffy teaches us that everyone has the potential for wrongdoing, and can also be redeemed. She knows that standing up to life is difficult and necessary. Demons can and will be beaten. Most importantly she knows to share her power and that you don't have to be the hero all the time. She believes that women can take on the world and that change is possible.

In business, an army of Truth Warriors defines the culture of the organization, their army. Cultures are created by the values we instill, the behaviours we reward and the systems we re-enforce. Armies of Truth Warriors value courage, risk taking but also compassion and trust. They reward the process, not just the outcome of decisions. They establish systems to challenge one another.

Leaders can create their army of Truth Warriors; they can build tribes with strength who define cultures of truth. They know they can't do it alone. They rally around a bigger purpose and make choices that support the goals they collectively want to achieve. They are humble and inclusive. An army of Truth Warriors can deliver success for individuals and organizations. They can change the world.

We need to make decisions that count for our WORLD.

On April 23, 2020, Donald Trump, the president of the United States, suggested in a live press conference that perhaps injecting disinfectant into the body could cure COVID-19. Barely eighteen hours after his public statement, the New York City Poison Control Center had received more than double its usual amount of calls, including nine people reporting exposure to Lysol, ten to bleach, and 11 who had been exposed to other household cleaners.

In 1998, British physician Andrew Wakefield published a study suggesting that the measles, mumps and rubella (MMR) vaccine, given to children around the age of 18 months and again at four years, could lead to autism. At the time of his study, measles was all but eradicated in the U.S., with only 86 confirmed cases in the year 2000. Celebrities endorsed Wakefield's message, and social media supported and spread it. Today, measles cases are on the rise and 54 percent of Americans believe that vaccines are unsafe. In 2019, the U.S. confirmed 1,282 cases of measles, despite the fact that Wakefield himself was discredited and subsequent research has indicated no link between vaccinations and autism.

The people who are poisoning themselves with disinfectant and making decisions about vaccinations on the basis of fraudulent information do so out of fear and blind faith. They do not stop to question it. Bad decisions cost lives. We are so committed to our own beliefs that instead of opening ourselves up to new information, we close up and dig in. We look for information to confirm our beliefs instead of looking for information to validate or deny them. The future depends on our ability to counteract this natural tendency. It requires that we pause and consider the possibility that our truth might not be the only truth and that our voice alone is not enough.

Our world is dividing. Science and scientists are struggling to convince other people to believe the truth. Those who have the facts often cannot clearly communicate them. Those who share their opinions with the world may be so convinced they're right that they have overlooked key facts. Both of these groups have the opportunity to *move* a different way.

We are surrounded by information but also misinformation. We have so much information that we cannot make sense of it. We struggle to distinguish between what is true and what is false. The decisions we make are becoming increasingly complex and yet the facts to make them are becoming more difficult to find.

We are living in a "me first" time, where the division between rich and poor has never been more pronounced. Facing this situation, our innate immediate response becomes one of self-preservation, leading to a heightened state of fear. This fear gets in the way of making better decisions. It forces us to hold more tightly to those beliefs that have shaped our experience. It stops us from speaking up or encourages us to speak so loudly that the thoughts of others are drowned out.

On a global scale, these mistakes cost lives. Decisions are being made with minimal thought and voices that should be heard are silenced. An article written by Jim Clifton in June 2019, before the pandemic of 2020, reported on answers to the question, "Do you trust science?" A substantial number of people (39 percent of respondents) answered "No" when asked if they trusted the government for medical advice. Clifton asked an even more important question: "What if trust in science and health crashed, so that when there is news of a potential pandemic, we just don't believe it?" The answer to this question played out in 2020, as death tolls rose in countries where governments doubted science and delayed action.

Resistance to scientific information and change has always existed. Ignaz Semmelweis was among the first doctors to promote handwashing. He was a Hungarian physician who worked in an obstetrical clinic. He discovered that mothers were dying of "childbed fever" at 2½ times the rate in a clinic overseen by medical students compared to the clinic where midwives were trained. The difference was due to the fact that the medical students were also working in a room where autopsies were carried out, and, Semmelweis suggested, were carrying "cadaverous particles" on their hands when they attended the mothers giving birth. (This was many years before Louis Pasteur advanced the germ theory of disease.) Semmelweis's introduction of antiseptic procedures reduced the mortality rate to below one percent. Despite evidence, the greater community did not believe him. He suffered a nervous breakdown and was sent to an asylum, where he died of injuries suffered at the hands of the guards.

Human beings resist change, and we react to those who contradict our long-held beliefs. We are shaped by our bias and experience. If we make better decisions, we enable change; change within ourselves and change within others.

"Social change begins with people getting out of themselves."
—Barack Obama

We can start small by questioning our beliefs and the decisions we make every day. We can respectfully challenge the decisions and embedded beliefs of others. Our decisions shape our beliefs, which shape our actions, which ultimately re-enforce our beliefs. It is an endless cycle that can be broken. If we build a world of Truth Warriors, we can rectify the poor mistakes of the past. It starts by understanding why we believe.

4. Why We Believe

We believe to support our cause.

During the winter months, I am typically at the hockey rink six days a week. I have three children that play and a husband that coaches. As the coach's wife, I am often privy to the differing opinions of the hockey parents in the stands. We disagree about which line is stronger or which goalie to play or what drills should be run in practice. We argue about fair play and who got longer shifts and who should have been benched. But there is one thing we can all agree on: the referees are against us. We are happy to yell out when the call seems unjust and provide reasoning to support why our player was unfairly treated. Yet we barely question the calls against the other team. The psychological term for this behaviour is motivated reasoning. We are seeking information that supports our desire to win. When the referee makes a call against our team, we scrutinize her decision and look for reasons for her to be wrong. Conversely, if she makes a call against the other team, we don't look too closely. I have seen some amazing ways in which hockey parents have justified poor behaviour.

In our hometown league, there are six associations that compete against one another. We compete on the ice and we compete for players off the ice. The result is that we know parents and kids on every team. On this particular evening, we were playing against a team whose coach used to coach our team and at least four of whose players had been previously been ours. My son is tall and lanky. He looks huge in his hockey equipment but probably weighs less than most of his opponents. Despite that fact, he normally throws himself in to the game. As a result, he gets and draws penalties equally. In this particular evening, he was scuffling with a boy in the corner. The boy fell and was clearly angered by the altercation. When he got up, he hit my son from behind, dropping him to his knees and then hit him in the back of the head with his stick. Had it not been on the ice, it would have been considered assault. The boy in question was penalized and suspended for future games. My son was diagnosed with a concussion and missed the rest of his hockey season. Although the incident itself was upsetting, it was not the most troubling for me. The other team knew my son and my family. Although they expressed concern, they did not acknowledge the inappropriate behaviour. Instead the coach on the other bench justified it by saying of the player who had just assaulted my son, "He's a good kid."

I also saw this type of motivated reasoning develop very early in my youngest hockey player. At the start of her hockey "career" the league set up a framework to promote the fun aspects of playing. In particular, they attempted to downplay winning and losing by not posting the score. But in her most recent season of hockey, they made a shift. The start of the year was for fun. They played on a shortened ice surface, with no penalties and no score. In January they shifted to what the parents would call "real" hockey. The refs were now making real calls and the score was officially posted. Almost immediately I saw the shift in both the coaches and the eight-year-old players. Arguing with the referees started almost immediately and the kids (having seen their official first loss) came off the ice blaming the ref for the bad game.

We believe to support our cause and often our cause is to win. In battle, we seek opinions to support our desired position and are biased towards winning. We are biased to overlook those beliefs or ideas that do not support our goals. One of the mistakes leaders often make is to focus too much on winning. A culture that stands together as one to challenge their competitors is an army of warriors. One that is pitted against one another with everyone striving to have the best idea or top performance will ultimately act in ways that lead to poorer decisions. Your contribution to a team should be motivated by making the best decision, not trying to work out who wins or loses.

When I was in sales, my aim was to grow revenue. I managed "spend" against my customers to deliver net sales—the closest visibility I had to bottom-line profit. The marketing team came to me with a proposed incentive that would drive volume. In this particular business, we sold single items and multipacks. Their incentive was a dollar discount off the single item. In my business, the multipacks out-sold the single packs by 10 times. I could see minimal benefit for me in spending money on promoting the single packs. When I challenged marketing's offer, they told me I needed to support sales of the single packs because they were more profitable for the company. Our goals were at odds. My targets were based on sales and the promotion didn't support my needs. Their targets were based on profit so they could not adjust their plan.

This happens all the time in organizations. Organizations are set up with naturally competing functions to allow the business to operate effectively. Sales would like an unlimited assortment of products, but the supply chain folks would prefer to produce fewer items. Marketing would like large budgets to fuel their brand growth, but Finance needs to grow the bottom line. Everyone would like more resources, but HR needs to manage the flow of people and change.

The opportunity is to find commonality across the organization—to focus on the long-term vision and goals. The key is to remove individual desire for the collective good. The end solution to my sales challenge was a long-term shift in our information and reward structure. The business began sharing costing information with the sales team and creating customer-level P&Ls to showcase the full profitability of our business. My colleagues and I were both targeted with bottom-line achievement. We came together with a common goal. We were set up to win together.

We believe in order to support our cause and to achieve our desired goals. By nature, human beings want to win. Truth Warriors are driven by this desire but use caution to avoid its traps. We need to avoid our personal desire to win at a cost of losing the overall battle. When we believe to support our cause, we become prone to try to validate that belief. We are bombarded with information and misinformation. What we believe is also necessary to simplify our view of the world.

We believe to simplify our world.

Walter White is a fictional character in the TV series *Breaking Bad*. If you have seen the show, you will understand the transformational journey he goes through. If you haven't seen the series and intend to do so, spoiler alert! The first episode introduces us to Walter White, a chemistry teacher, working part-time in a car wash, who has just been diagnosed with lung cancer. He embarks on selling meth to provide money for his family after his death. The end of the first episode leaves us with Walt in his underwear, crying as he believes the police are about to arrest him. He pulls the trigger, trying to kill himself, but it misfires. He awaits his arrest, only to discover that the police are not in fact looking for him. He lives to cook another day. We, the audience, are happy that he survived. We see him as a victim and not as a criminal.

Throughout the early episodes, Walt tells himself and others that he is only making meth to help his family. His health and financial situation allow him to justify his behaviour. Initially, the people he ends up hurting are the "bad guys." It is obvious in the beginning of the series that Walt is uncomfortable with his behaviour. In the second episode, he takes a man hostage and decides to let him go rather than to kill him. (Unfortunately, his trust is betrayed, the man tries to kill him, and Walt is required to kill him in return.)

As the series progresses, Walt begins to behave (and believe) much more like a criminal and less like the victim. He becomes enamoured with his power and commits acts of violence, deception and treachery that we would not have thought possible of the Walt we met in episode 1. He had to adjust his beliefs to accommodate his behaviour.

What he experienced is what psychologists call cognitive dissonance. People strive for internal consistency. We don't like it when we experience conflict with what we believe, and we look to reduce this discomfort. To do so, we change our beliefs to more closely align with how we acted.

We struggle when our beliefs are challenged. We prefer to mitigate this discomfort by seeking out information that confirms our pre-existing beliefs or preconceptions. This is called confirmation bias. The result of confirmation bias is that we hold strong to our beliefs and shut down any challenge that might lead to alternative possibilities. We are so strong in our need to be consistent in our beliefs that we forget to consider the accuracy of them. In decision-making, this causes us to ignore information that might actually be useful in making the best possible decision.

When we believe something, we are likely to continue to believe it and we look for information to support it. Social media thrives on confirmation bias. Algorithms exist to show us information that aligns to our beliefs. If you were a Trump supporter, you were likely to see information about the wonderful things he has done for the country. If you were not a Trump supporter, you were likely to see information about all the lies he has told. And just like the referee who makes a call against the team we are cheering for, we will probably ignore or explain away information that goes against our belief.

Much of what we believe is shaped by bias and simple heuristics. A heuristic is a mental shortcut that allows people to solve problems and make judgments quickly and efficiently. These rule-of-thumb strategies shorten decision-making time and allow people to function without constantly stopping to think about their next course of action. Daniel Kahneman won the Nobel prize in economics for his work on heuristics and bias, and in his book *Thinking Fast & Slow*, he talks about the many ways in which we rely on these tools to simplify our world—often to our detriment.

He recommends counterbalancing these biases is through recognition and purposeful effort. When we are tired (cognitively lazy or physically so), we are more likely to not recognize the biases that are foundational to our existence. We need to acknowledge and pay attention to avoid what comes naturally. Kahneman states:

> When you are in a state of cognitive ease, you are probably in a good mood, like what you see, believe what you hear, trust your intuitions. You are also likely to be relatively casual and superficial in your thinking. When you feel strained, you are more likely to be vigilant and suspicious, invest more effort in what you are doing, feel less comfortable and make fewer errors.

He illustrates this point by sharing a study that was carried out on 40 Princeton students. They were asked to complete a small test. Half of them were shown the question in normal font, the other half in a barely legible font. Which group do you believe were more likely to make a mistake? Ninety percent of students reading the normal font made a mistake while only 35 percent of those reading the barely legible test made a mistake. By paying closer attention, we make fewer mistakes.

Many of the beliefs we have and decisions we make are subconscious. Most of our behaviours are carried out without our truly understanding why we do what we do. Marketers have understood and leveraged this reality of human behaviour for years. Can you remember the sound that Netflix makes when it starts up or the Intel "sounder" on computer commercials? These companies have imprinted a sound on your mind, one that makes you think of a particular brand. We are no better than Pavlov's dog in responding to cues. And although those cues simplify our lives, they also stop us from making better decisions.

We reject information that is more complex or goes against our current beliefs, but we also tune out information we should potentially pay attention to. In 1996, Daniel Simons and Christopher Chabris conducted a study to demonstrate how easily we miss information we are not actively seeking. As part of the study, they showed participants a video that you can find on my website. Before you read further, watch the video yourself and see how you do on the test.

Did you spot the gorilla? This study illustrates attention bias; the human tendency to pay attention to some things while simultaneously ignoring others. We become so focused on detecting a specific object that we look past an obvious odd intrusion. If we can miss something so obviously wrong in a short video, what are we missing in our daily lives?

"Facts are stubborn things, but our minds are even more stubborn."
—John Adams

Our world is complex. In order to navigate it, we need to make it simpler. When we act in a way that goes against our values, we shift our beliefs. We also reject information that does not conform to our existing beliefs and overlook information that might result in a different opinion. Our busy lives prevent us from investigating alternatives. Just as Walter White transformed his beliefs based on his behaviour, we can do the same. We cannot prevent the biases that come naturally, but Truth Warriors can acknowledge their existence, attempt to recognize them and move differently to correct for them. In doing so, we must also be careful not to trust the information from others too much.

We believe because we trust others too much.

I once saw a video called "Dinosaur Hoax: Fossils." You can watch it for yourself on YouTube. It provides what seems to be facts that suggest that dinosaur fossils are actually a made-up phenomenon perpetuated to support millions of dollars in scientific research funding. The woman in the video tells us that fossils are actually rocks and that paleontologists took these rocks to reconstruct what they believed to be bones from dinosaurs. Her primary argument was this:

The first fossil that was ever found was actually found after they came up with the idea of a dinosaur.

I found this compelling. If true, it suggested that paleontologists were looking for fossils to support their belief that dinosaurs existed. When they uncovered a rock that could be formed into a bone, they did so. They reconstructed the dinosaur based on their belief and no other evidence. They started with a picture of what the dinosaur was supposed to look like and pieced together rocks to support their perception. Their jobs and millions of dollars were on the line, leading them to reproduce what they believed to be true.

This short video had me question my long-held belief that dinosaurs existed. It was a well-constructed argument. Unfortunately, the primary fact supporting her argument was not true. I immediately Googled "when did we discover the first dinosaur bone" and came to an article stating this fact:

Even early scientists weren't sure about the fossils they found. For example, in 1676, Reverend Robert Plot, a curator of an English museum, discovered a large thigh bone in England. He believed it belonged to ancient species of human "giants."

As it turns out, fossilized bones were found long before the concept of dinosaurs existed. Almost one million people saw that video. How many also took the time to validate the facts behind her argument? How many just believed what the video told them, and shifted their beliefs about science based on a three-minute video? We are too quick to trust our own understanding of what we hear. Children, in particular, inherently trust everything they hear.

A few years ago, my oldest son and I were taking a trip to the store. He was on his scooter and I was walking along beside him. I remarked to him about how the scooter was a "smart" purchase since he got a lot of use out of it. He froze and said, "I thought Santa got me this scooter." I stopped and considered my blunder. I tried to cover up my mistake. "Ummmm…. I thought I bought that for you for your birthday." He responded promptly with "No, it was from Christmas. Are you Santa Claus?" The question caught me off guard. He was 11 years old at the time, so the question itself was not surprising, but the timing threw me off. I attempted a feeble "What do you believe?" but quickly confessed.

For those who celebrate Christmas, the concept of Santa Claus is a widely held belief. As parents we instil and reinforce this belief in our children. So why do kids believe in Santa Claus? It starts with the fact that they trust the people who are telling them these stories. At a young age, children trust their parents implicitly. As they age and friends present conflicting advice, they start to question who they trust more. As their brains develop, the rational side of their thought process questions the logistics of Santa Claus. I struggled with this concept the most. When I found out that Santa wasn't real, I was intent on keeping it from my younger sister. I started to stockpile all the answers to her potential questions. I am not a good liar, so I had to be prepared to play my part in this cover-up. I thought she would ask about how he comes down the chimney or visits so many houses in one night. I prepared my answers. She never asked. She just believed! She had no need to question her beliefs. She was benefiting from Santa Claus. Her family was telling her it was true. There was no need to question it. Many of our beliefs are like this. If we trust the teller, if the impact is beneficial, we don't need much else.

Most of us trust doctors and we look to them for advice. When I had my first child and was trying to get him to sleep on his own, I asked my family doctor about what he recommended. He talked to me about "Ferberizing," a very popular method of letting your child "cry it out." Although I desperately wanted to get a good night's sleep, I also didn't feel I had it in me to listen to my child cry. I took to the literature. Many parenting books and two children later, I realize now that his advice was his opinion and only one of many alternatives.

The learning for me is that there are no surefire solutions to getting your kids to sleep.. There are lots of techniques you can try but each child is different. Each family is different. The doctor may be an expert in many things, but he is not an expert in my case, or my history, or my values. He might suggest a "cry it out" routine that I couldn't execute or a bottle that my child did not like. Should I rely on his expertise on whether to vaccinate my children? Absolutely. Should I consider his perspective on whether my son needs antibiotics for an ear infection? Of course. We need to leverage the expertise of others but we also need to be willing to respectfully challenge their beliefs, either directly or through our own research.

I am not suggesting that we shouldn't trust others or experts in their fields. In fact, I believe one of the main ways to make better decisions is through trust. Truth Warriors need to avoid blind trust. They must consider carefully what others have to say and the context in which they say it. Different people, different groups, and different cultures have different people they implicitly believe. Canadians are more apt to blindly believe what the government tells us, whereas our American neighbours are not. Some cultures believe strongly in Western science while others believe more in spiritual guidance. Whom we implicitly believe isn't as important as the fact that all groups have the tendency to blindly believe someone. We don't have to be critics but we all have an opportunity to be more critical in our thinking. We can critically question the world around us. Just as we must be careful not to trust others too much, we must also be careful not to trust ourselves too much.

We believe because we trust ourselves too much.

In 2003, Phil Tetlock published a book called *Expert Political Judgement: How Good Is It? How Can We Know?* He reviewed 82,361 predictions over the course of more than 20 years against their correlation to success. He could not find any correlation between education and experience. Newbies did just as well as highly experienced individuals. Ph.D.'s performed just as well as those without. The only correlation he did find was that those experts who made more media appearances tended to be worse predictors.

Media presence ties to ego. The more inflated your ego, the more likely you are to believe in your expertise and de-value the opinions of others. Another study, conducted by Haywad and Hambrick, tested the egos of CEOs against their spend on acquisitions (a very costly investment). The measure of ego was based on media praise, recent strong performance and the pay gap between them and the next highest paid officer of the company. They discovered that those who had bigger egos paid more for acquisitions than those with lower egos. They erroneously believed that an acquisition was worth more, simply because they thought themselves more capable in acquiring it. For each article favourable to the CEO, the purchase price increased by $4.8 million.

Expertise and intelligence do not make you immune to bias. As you become skilled in a task, its demand for energy diminishes. Your perceived expertise stops you from paying attention. Even those without an over-inflated ego or high media exposure are not immune. Psychologists call this overconfidence bias—the tendency to hold a false and misleading assessment of our skills, intellect, or talent.

Truth Warriors understand that they are not infallible or immune to bias. They are confident but skeptical of their own beliefs. They recognize that decision-making should be not effortless and that their expertise can contribute to a validation of their own truth, but that it does not necessarily represent the collective truth.

Like truth, our beliefs are not static. They are not immovable. To challenge our beliefs, Truth Warriors do two things: first, seeks to understand and second, to speak the truth even when it is difficult to do. This is the dance we need to do.

5. The Dance of the Truth Warrior

During the COVID pandemic, I was fortunate enough to hear Geeta Sankappanavar speak as part of the "Canada's Most Powerful Women" roundtable. Geeta is a woman of colour working in a highly dominated male industry (oil and gas). She was living in New York City in 2001 on 9/11. She helped lead her company through this crisis and later did the same during the 2008 financial crisis. She shared her insight on the current crisis and how leaders need to think differently about how to tackle it. She was fascinating to listen to but what impressed me most was that she began her 10-minute dialogue by saying, "I need to first start by telling you about me. You need to know the personal bias I bring to this discussion. You need to understand the lens someone sees the world from before you believe them."

We believe what we believe because we see and hear what we want to see and hear. We ignore information that does not suit our purpose and pay more attention to information that suits our existing perceptions. We trust ourselves a little too much and are drawn in by small bits of information from others that we trust or that fits with our existing beliefs.

Just like truth, our beliefs are fluid and personal. We hold dear to our beliefs as a part of who we are. They become part of our identity instead of part of a debate. We focus on who is right and who is wrong instead of what is and what might be. When we are contradicted, our natural biases cause us to stay firm when in fact we should allow ourselves to move. When our beliefs are strong, we need more than ever to consider alternatives. We need to pause, recognize our bias and look for ways to counterbalance them.

> "When your beliefs are entwined with your identity, changing your mind means changing your identity. That's a really hard sell."
> —Al Gore, An Inconvenient Truth

The most common dance of the Warrior is the Haka. The first Hakas were created and performed by different Māori tribes of New Zealand as a war dance. It was traditionally used to prepare for battle, as a demonstration of courage and strength. It was performed either on the battlefield prior to engagement with the enemy, or as the war party was leaving their own village enroute to a battle. Today, the Haka has evolved as a dance of both togetherness and individuality. It is a way for communities to come together, symbolizing unity and strength. Within this framework it allows for freedom of expression and is more inclusive.

The Truth Warrior of today embodies the essence of the Haka. There are four key elements that define any dance: space, time, energy and action. Space describes how dancers interact with the world around them. They can stay in place or move from one place to another. They may alter direction and pathways. They can focus their movement inwards or outwards. They can be direct in their line of travel or slow and meandering. Space plays an equally important part in uncovering the truth and making decisions. Those who seek truth can do so by looking inwards or outwards. They can make decisions in an instant or in a purposeful, structured manner.

Time best describes the "when" or rhythm of the dance. Movements are timed to be simultaneous or sequential, brief or long, fast or slow, predictable or unpredictable. Dancers take cues from each other or from external events such as a whistle or drum beat. The same applies to truth and decisions. Those who seek truth know how to see the movement in others. They know how to *move* with others.

Energy is about how the movement happens. It includes the use of force, tension and weight. It might be free flowing or easily stopped, tight or loose, heavy or light, powerful or gentle. Energy may change in an instant. It will also reveal the emotion of the dance with either a powerful push or a playful nudge. Energy highly influences truth and decisions. Those who speak truth know to balance their message; when to be gentle and when to be more powerful. They use their energy for good. They influence and do not coerce.

Action is any movement dancers take. However, it not only refers to steps and sequences but also to pauses and moments of relative stillness. It is knowing when to advance and when to retreat. Those who lead truth know when to pause and when to push forward. They know when to prepare for battle and when to retreat and restock.

Truth is a dance and Truth Warriors are the dancers. They interact in a changing world. They can choose to look outwards or inwards, move quickly or slowly. They can rely on others or search within themselves. They can use force to get their message across or be minimal in their movements.

The Truth Warrior tribe is one of togetherness but also of individual bravery. Becoming a Truth Warrior is not about a lone fight. It is about a battle of interconnection. The interconnection of our various truths. Making decisions is about finding the best solution among our various truths. It is about being less wrong in our understanding of the world. Finding the best solution involves pinpointing the truth—or the closest thing to it. If we are to be confident in our decisions, we need to feel that we are basing them on the best truth of the moment but we also need to recognize that they can change. Our experience of yesterday does not necessarily reflect the experience of tomorrow. My truth will be different than yours and we both have assumptions that shape our beliefs. We can all move towards a new truth. We can all make better decisions. Only through this battle can we achieve peace.

PART TWO

Seek Truth: Balancing Rational and Intuitive

6. Finding the Balance

In 1994, Jeff Bezos came across a staggering fact. The World Wide Web, which at the time most people had never heard of, was growing at a rate of around 2300 percent per year. He recognized that this level of growth indicated the potential for something bigger. He knew there was a business idea there. He then came up with potential opportunities and force-ranked them against specific criteria. He focused on books because there were substantially more items in this category than any others he considered. His idea was to create universal access to books; at that time even the largest Barnes & Noble "superstore" stocked less than 150,000 unique titles. Smaller stores only carried 10,000-30,000 unique titles. And that was how Amazon was born.

The decision started with rational thought, grounded in the facts of the internet's growth and the opportunity for book sales. It was led by fact, supported by criteria, and executed with thought. But ultimately Bezos claims that the decision was made with his heart. He had to take a risk and trust his instinct. When he first told his wife about his idea her first question was, "What's the internet?" Given the completely unknown nature of this concept at the time, he needed to rely on his "gut" to tell him it was worth trying. He did what great decision-makers do—balance intuitive and rational thought.

Seeking truth starts with a willingness to understand. It requires searching out data that both supports and contradicts your idea. It involves recognizing the mistakes of the past and considering the implications of mistakes in the future. It requires diversity of thought and the opinions of others.

In battle, whether in the military or corporate arena, we seek opinions to support our desired direction. We are biased to overlook beliefs or ideas that do not support our goals. We may play the role of Soldier before the role of Scout. The Soldier focuses on how to win and defends her ideas. She is influenced by motivated reasoning and does not challenge her beliefs. Conversely, the Scout's goal is not to win or lose, but to understand. Seeking truth is about pausing to understand.

How we seek to understand is done in different ways. We are inclined to rely on fact or instinct depending on how we make decisions. The rational truth seeker is one who uses reason and logic to support their ideas. They are more likely to make decisions based on a structured sequence of steps, supported by facts and analysis. These decisions are often sound and tested, but also take longer to make. The intuitive truth seeker is one who looks to experience to support their ideas. They are more likely to make decisions based on experiences in the past, feelings and accumulated judgment. Both have validity and both are necessary, although both also have challenges associated with them.

7. The Rational Truth Seeker

Lisa was a coaching client who wanted to focus on making better decisions. She was a new manager, with only about two years of experience in having a team reporting to her. She had been given a lot of additional responsibilities to lead her department, which was the only one in the company that was growing. It was expected to be the key driver behind the business. She was getting feedback that she wasn't making decisions fast enough. She had a manager who was very quick to make decisions and constantly threw ideas Lisa's way that she was expected to act on. She was feeling overwhelmed.

As the coaching engagement continued, we began to talk through different personality styles—those of Lisa, her manager, and other executives in the business. It quickly became obvious that her profile was very different from those of the other leaders. Her approach was much more collaborative; her need for facts much greater. Her decision-making style was much more rational than those she reported to.

As a result, her decisions were perceived to be slow. Other executives would throw something at her and she would be expected to respond by the end of the day. This just didn't feel comfortable for her. She knew it was important to consider all the options, and that she would like to involve all the stakeholders. But those above her wanted a decision *now*.

As part of our coaching, we spoke about the benefits of her approach—what she thought she brought to business by being "slower" than everyone else. We spoke about how her team perceived her as a leader. Her team, in fact, confirmed through a 360 review that she was the best leader they had ever had. They raved about the amount of collaboration and support they got.

Eventually she started to see the benefits of her decision-making process. She was helping others in the business to validate their thinking. She was supporting and engaging her team. It was slower, but it was effective. Now the challenge was to convince the leaders above her to allow her to be different. Her job was to show them the benefit of her rational style while at the same time recognizing the need for her to adapt.

In the process of our coaching, Lisa realized that her decision style was not wrong but also that the perception of it had to change. She also realized that she could not hold tight to her style in every instance. She had to show willingness to let go of her need to obtain all the facts or to collaborate. She had to have confidence that her experience and her intuition were guiding her properly. She had to do the dance of the Truth Warrior, knowing when to speed up and when to slow down. She took cues from the other dancers.

The transformation for Lisa began by acknowledging her unique perspective and the different perspectives and approaches of her team and manager. The 360 review helped her to see that her team valued her style and helped Lisa to see the benefit of her diversity. This built confidence. As Lisa began to trust in herself, she was better able to explain the benefit to the executives. The 360 review also helped her to see the implications of her style for the company's leaders. This allowed her to move a different way when required. She would provide detailed timelines that would allow her time to gather the information she needed and she worked hard to let go when the deadline came. If it didn't feel like she had enough information, she still needed to make the decision.

The rational decision maker has a role to play in helping to validate decisions. They are the PAUSE button for the organization. They are the Scout in battle who helps to identify potential obstacles. The biggest risk of this decision style is inaction. Rational decision makers often get paralyzed by their inability to decide without having all the facts. The biggest fear for this type of decision maker is regret. Studies show that regret plays a large role in how we make decisions, to the point of rewarding inaction over action.

Miller and Taylor conducted a study to understand the relation of regret to inaction. The study simulated a game of blackjack where participants played against a computer. There were two different groups being tested. Both groups were given the same cards, with the same opportunities to win and lose. The only difference between the groups was how they were asked if they wanted another card. One group was asked "Do you want to hit?" while the other was asked "Do you wish to stand?" When they lost, the participants were asked to measure their level of regret. Those answering the question "Do you want to hit?" expressed much stronger regret when they lost than those asked if they wished to stand. We feel less regret when we avoid acting and more regret when we take an action that leads to a poor outcome. We prefer inaction over action.

To not make a decision is a decision. However, it is not always the best one. Allowing time for more information puts the rational decision maker at risk. My husband, the hockey coach, needs to make a choice every year on who will make our A-level team. Although there are official tryouts, the process in reality is much more informal. As the season winds down, the coach will talk to the players he knows he wants back next year. He will unofficially offer them a spot on next year's team. All the players and parents know this is how the game works and recognize that if the coach hasn't spoken to them yet, they are at risk of not making the team (or, as we call it, "on the bubble"). As a result, they often check with other comparable teams to see if they can land a spot there. The risk for the coach in deciding the team roster is who to talk to and when. He knows that if he does not commit to a player, he risks losing them to another team. He also knows that if he commits to a player, he fills a spot that might otherwise go to a stronger player that is considering his team. The timing of everyone's decisions makes the process very difficult to manoeuvre.

An engineer by profession, my husband is primarily a rational decision maker. He takes the decision about who will be on the team extremely seriously. Knowing the impact of getting cut on a young player, he wants to make sure he is fair and accurate in his process. He considers many factors in deciding who to commit to and who to put on the bubble. A few years back, he struggled in deciding about a particular player who was a great kid but was having trouble keeping up with the pace of the game. My husband was not convinced that the player was right for the team and spoke to both the player and his parent about what he needed to do to up his game. The player did up his game: in the next two games, his effort increased substantially. It made my husband re-consider his initial perspective. He still wasn't sure and wanted more data and more time and more proof. He watched him for three more games before he became convinced that the player was capable. He offered him a spot. The player declined, having found another team that saw his potential.

My husband's rational style enabled him to carefully consider his decision but also stopped him from deciding fast enough. His need for more information stopped him from acting, and as a result he did not get the outcome he had hoped for. He had the opportunity to go with his intuition but chose differently.

The rational truth seeker offers many benefits to an organization. They are great validators and the facts and logic they bring to decision-making help support a solid decision. These truth seekers must balance the need for speed against the need for information. They need to know when to let go of the need for enough information and move another way. They must recognize that sometimes we need *less* information.

8. Why We Need Less Information

We need less information because we are overwhelmed.

Draeger's is an upscale grocery store in California that focuses on creating a food experience for its customers. They pride themselves on the variety they offer, boasting 250 different kinds of mustards and vinegars, over 500 different kinds of fruits and vegetables, and 348 different varieties of jam. Sheena Iyengar is a professor of business in the Management Department at Columbia Business School and is known for her expertise in choice. She shares her experience as a graduate student as she tested the implications of such a wide range of choices on the decisions made by the shoppers at Draeger's. In her TED talk "How to make choosing easier" she describes the results. Two different test cases were set up. In one scenario, six varieties of jam were available for shoppers to choose from, and in another there were 24 varieties. The result of the experiment? More people stopped to sample the jams when there were 24 varieties to choose from, but fewer people actually bought a jar. When there were 24 choices, only three percent of shoppers made a purchase. When there were six choices, 30 percent did.

Sheena did further research and identified three main negative consequences of offering people more choice:

1. They're more likely to delay choosing and to procrastinate even when doing so goes against their best interests.
2. They're more likely to make worse choices.

3. They're more likely to choose things that make them less satisfied, even when the products objectively perform better.

An overabundance of information can actually be a detriment to decision making. Ultimately, we make worse decisions and are less satisfied when we have too many choices. One of the techniques Sheena shared is what she calls a "condition for complexity." This time, she set up an experiment with two situations in which people needed to make a decision. Participants were building a custom car from scratch with 60 different decisions to be made, each with its own set of choices. One group made easy decisions first. The other started with more difficult decisions. Both groups had the same information and decisions to make. What varied was the order in which they made them. What she found was that people were more engaged and capable when they started with easy decisions first. Those who first had to choose from four options for the gear-shift lever and then went on to harder decisions (like choosing from 56 options for paint colour) were more likely to stick with the process than those who went through it in the opposite direction.

When seeking truth, we need to be careful not to overload ourselves and our teams with information. We need to begin more broadly and simply. Although brainstorming can be an effective start to define a problem or solution alternatives, we need to narrow the list quickly and with a broader purpose in mind. We need to understand our audience. We need to avoid temptation to overload others with facts when challenging their beliefs. We need less information to simplify matters and get our message across to others.

> **We need less information to get our message across.**

In my career in sales I had the opportunity to call on two of the biggest Canadian retailers—first Loblaws, followed by Walmart. In my meetings with the Loblaws buyer, I would come prepared with my presentation decks full of facts, ready to convince him of my solution. The presentation was full of numbers and I would circle the numbers that were most relevant to my message. I put a big headline at the top of each slide with my main message. I had lots of data to prove my point. What I didn't count on was the fact that the buyer had his own agenda. He looked at all my data points, called out a particular number in one of my tables, and asked me, "Why is that area in decline?" I stammered because I hadn't researched every number on the slides myself. I didn't know the answer. I had presented a whole bunch of facts, but did not have enough understanding of the buyer's area of focus to realize that he would zoom in on something that I had deemed "irrelevant." I had to tell him that I didn't know the answer but that I would research the matter further and get back to him. Of course, at the next meeting I came prepared with the answer to that question and some new sets of facts. Once again, he challenged me, this time on my new set of numbers. It didn't take me long to realize that I had to either know the reasons behind *every* number I presented, or leave them off completely. The buyer's desire for detail matched my own and if I were to be successful, I had to prepare accordingly.

My experience with the buyer at Walmart was entirely different. That buyer was much more intuitive in her decision making. She had been buying for that category for years and had massive amounts of experience she could rely on to make decisions. She was not at all interested in my fresh-faced "facts." I prepared my PowerPoint deck: key facts only, headings to support my message, clear flow and logic behind every page. I started to walk her through it. She took the printed copy of the presentation from my hand, flipped to the middle—the page where I proposed a price for a promotion after much logic about why she should do it—and wrote a new, lower price on the page. "Give me this price and I'll do the promotion," she said. "Thanks for the meeting."

I stared at her with my mouth agape. I didn't know how to respond. I didn't have the authority to make the decision right there about a price reduction, or frankly the data to justify it to her or me. I had to thank her for her time and tell her I would follow up. She and I worked together for two more years after that. I learned how to navigate between my natural propensity for facts and her quick intuitive decisions. Both had value. I reduced my presentation decks substantially, sometimes to just a page or two to cover the issues I knew were important to her. She appreciated the efficiency and as my experience grew and I was able to prove that I had a better understanding of her business, she trusted me to propose the right solutions. She still didn't need the facts from me. She knew the facts already. She needed to know that I understood her business, that I understood her, and that she and I were working towards the same goals.

When our beliefs are challenged, it is human nature to defend our position. We aim to counterattack with facts to support our argument. Ironically, when we ourselves believe in something strongly, alternative facts fail to change our perspective unless we are purposeful in being receptive to them.

Truth Warriors need to be able to flex their fact muscles and move up and down in their depth of data depending on their audience. Rational truth seekers are often tempted to demonstrate a depth of knowledge. If they do this to someone who doesn't appreciate or understand the facts, they will cause them to turn away. The key to using data to support an argument is to ensure its relevance and know when to let go of your need for "all the information."

The Intuitive Truth Seeker has a different challenge.

9. The Intuitive Truth Seeker

As a teenager, Chester Carlson developed an interest in both chemistry and the written word. He brought these passions together when he obtained a small printing press and printed a few issues of a magazine aimed at amateur chemists. This first experience illustrated to him the challenge in making multiple copies of written documents. It began a lifelong journey into the process of duplication.

This passion continued at his first job at Bell Labs where he was responsible for making copies of patent specifications and drawings. The methods in use at the time involved retyping the document or creating a carbon copy. Both were time consuming. Mimeographs, which used "wet copying" technology, were more expensive and relied on the use of chemicals.

After being fired from Bell Labs, Carlson started working at the P. R. Mallory Company (known today as Duracell). He was leading the patent team during the day and studying law in the evening. Because he could not afford to buy the books required for his education, he had to copy the texts by hand. In his job, he continued to use the same challenging methods he used at Bell Labs. The labour required to achieve both these tasks set Carlson on a path to find a better way.

In his own kitchen, Carlson began to experiment with copying methods using light. He came across an article by Pal Selenyi that set out the fundamental principles of using ions to create an electrostatic charge. This would become a process Carlson called electrophotography, combining electrostatic printing with photography. To further his research he set up a small lab and hired an unemployed young physicist, a German refugee named Otto Kornei. It was here that xerography was invented—in Greek, "xeros" means "dry" and "graphia" means "writing," emphasizing the fact that unlike other re-production techniques, this process used no liquid chemicals.

Fearful that others might be blazing the same trail as he, Carl-son carefully patented his ideas as he learned more about this new technology. His fear was unfounded. Carlson spent the next five years searching for a company to develop his invention. After being turned down by more than twenty companies, Carlson entered into an agreement with a small called Haloid, which made and sold pho-tographic paper. Joseph C. Wilson had just assumed leadership of the company from his father. Its earnings were shrinking and market share was in decline.

Like Carlson, Haloid struggled to find people interested in the new technology. They demonstrated the process at a Detroit meet-ing of the American Optical Society on October 22, 1948, ten years to the day after Carlson created the first xerographic image. Society members were interested, but couldn't see how this crude process offered any particular advantage. Wilson worried about the amount of investment required to bring the project to life. In the end, Wilson had to decide whether to proceed with a product that no one could say would either work or sell. He decided to take the risk.

In 1959, Haloid took a gamble in launching the first office copier using xerography. They expected 5,000 units would be sold over the next three years. Instead, within two years 10,000 had been shipped and soon orders were backlogged. They had estimated that a typi-cal customer would make approximately 2,000 copies a month, but many made 10,000 and some even made 100,000 copies. The com-pany's name was later changed to Xerox, which also became a com-mon way of referring to the process of photocopying itself

Carlson went on to win many awards for his invention, includ-ing Inventor of the Year in 1964. His original patent can be seen on display in the Smithsonian Institution. Joseph C. Wilson later said, "We learned that great rewards come to those who see needs that have not been clearly identified by others, and who have the innovat-ing capacity to devise products and services which fill these needs."

At the time of launch, no one was asking for this type of product. Customers told Haloid that they did not see the need. But Carlson's experience with the current copying methods had led him to believe that the benefit was there. His intuition was telling him what the facts were not—that he had a product that would succeed.

> "Intuition is a very powerful thing, more powerful than intellect, in my opinion." —Steve Jobs

Intuition has a role to play in our decisions and those who use it can move more quickly —and, often, into uncharted territory. The risk for this kind of decision-maker is their sole reliance on intuition. It is possible to fool ourselves into thinking we have seen a given situation before and that our experience will help us make a sound decision. Circumstances change constantly, which means we need to evaluate each challenge. The executive who declares "I have been running this company for 30 years and I know what will work and not work" really believes that her experience will help make the right decision. But she is not considering changes in the environment the company operates in when she relies only on her own experience to make a decision. She will not have been exposed to how a problem might have been solved in other companies.

Xerox itself later struggled with this problem. Although known as an innovator because of the wildly successful development and roll-out of the office copier, Xerox later struggled to gain traction with many of their other inventions. They invented the laser printer, the graphical user interface for personal computers, and the computer mouse, but failed to commercialize and capitalize on these. Instead, Xerox relied on its past model of success. Mark B. Myers, a former senior vice-president of research and technology at Xerox, explained: "Xerox focused on businesses that had extremely high profit margins, rather than those that had rapid turns characteristic of low-margin businesses," he says. The result was that Xerox all but abandoned the laser-printer field to rivals like Hewlett-Packard.

Eventually Xerox recognized that its current model would not suit new business opportunities and, under the leadership of Richard Thoman, re-organized the sales force and billing system. Unfortunately, the execution of this did not go well. George Day, the director of Wharton's Emerging Technologies Research Management Program, points out that Thoman "was aggressive and quick to make decisions, but he did not have the support of key members within the company." Gabriel Szulanksi, who teaches management at Wharton, says Xerox got into trouble with its reorganization efforts because it tried to force through changes without adequate preparation. They had assumed that their past experience would lead to equal success.

The Intuitive truth-seeker can offer many benefits to an organization. They bring creativity and new ideas. They are more likely to take risks and move quickly, but need to ensure their ideas are valid. Intuition needs to be balanced with careful thought on the implications to the decision. Intuitive decision makers need to be careful to challenge their own beliefs and recognize that the experience of the past may not be suitable for the decisions of the future. Sometimes they need more information.

10. Why We Need More Information

B elow is a list of facts and myths. Before we begin, take a minute to indicate which are true (facts) and which are false (myths):

> **We need more information to compensate for blind spots.**

1. Adding a sprinkle of salt to water makes it boil faster.
2. Napoleon was shorter than average.
3. You can see the Great Wall of China from the moon.
4. The water in a flushed toilet rotates the other way in Australia.
5. Einstein failed math.
6. We have five senses.
7. If you touch a baby bird, their mother will abandon it.
8. Alcohol kills brain cells.
9. There are different sections of the tongue for each taste.
10. Humans use only 10 percent of their brain.
11. It's dangerous to waken a sleepwalker.
12. Bananas grow on trees.
13. Bats are blind.
14. Caffeine dehydrates you.
15. Goldfish have a three-second span of memory.
16. Shaving makes hair thicker.
17. It takes seven years to digest gum.
18. Sugar leads to hyperactivity in children.
19. Bulls hate the colour red.
20. Hair and nails keep growing after death.

If you believed any of these statements to be true, you would be wrong. Each is a myth. Thankfully, these are harmless examples of widely held beliefs that are not true. For a more alarming view of misinformation, I encourage you to read Hans Rosling's book *Factfulness*. He offers numerous examples of assumptions we have made about the world that are simply not true. You can take the "Factfulness Quiz" yourself and test your understanding of more important long-held beliefs.

We need more information to challenge our pre-existing beliefs and to circumvent our blind spots. We have to be open to recognizing how many of our own long-held beliefs are not based on any evidence. Just because we have believed something for a long time or because a lot of other people believe it, doesn't mean it is true. Both the rational and intuitive truth seeker can gather information. The former is more likely to do so with data and numbers and the latter will draw on their experience and the experiences of others. Understanding truth is not just about analyzing data. It is also understanding the environment you work in, through listening.

We all have bias and blind spots that shape our thinking. To understand your blind spots, check out "Project Implicit." It is an ongoing study conducted by Harvard that will identify your implicit beliefs on race, gender and sexual orientation. I was surprised—and somewhat dismayed—by my own results. To compensate for biases, we all need to first acknowledge they exist. By gathering more information, we can fill the holes in our blind spots. We can look for information that not only validates our beliefs, but challenges them. This will allow us to expand our understanding.

We need more information to expand our understanding.

I spoke with an intuitive leader about how he gathers information. When he takes on a new team or project, he starts with a roadshow. He travels for three weeks and speaks to everyone in the business. He asks them about their spouses, their kids, their hobbies. In the last 15 minutes of the conversation, they give him a small nugget of information about their area of the business that helps to shape his direction. He doesn't write anything down. At the end of his journey, he puts together the nuggets in his head and has a good understanding of the problem he needs to solve. His model enables the collective truth of others.

We need information from experts. In this particular example, the experts worked in the business and could provide insight into the challenges and opportunities facing it. In other situations, the experts are those who have a deep understanding of a specific issue. They may be doctors or scientists or analysts. In the course of the COVID-19 pandemic, the question of expert opinion as opposed to public opinion came to the forefront. One of my favourite examples was a post on Reddit in a discussion about mask wearing. As one commenter put it, "So because the CDC said it, you're just going to blindly listen to them without doing your own research?" A user responded to her question:

> YES. 100% YES YES YES. What f**king research am I going to do that is going to in any way be more valid or valuable than research from a government agency that spends $6.5 BILLION a year on studying diseases? Do you honestly think your Google skills are worth six and half billion dollars a year of scientific research by scientists specially [sic] in that field? You listen to the CDC when they say how to handle a pandemic. Period.

We need information to challenge our beliefs. We need to recognize that our experience is limited and rely on the experience and expertise of others. Information is the doorway to a better understanding of our world and our choices. We need to sift through misinformation and supplement it with facts. Without it, we may live in fear.

We need more information to combat fear.

On March 11, 2020 the World Health Organization declared the spread of COVID-19 to be a pandemic. Almost immediately, I felt afraid. I know I was not alone in this fear. The world faced the same uncertainty. I was afraid for our financial security. I was the sole provider at the time and my business was at risk. More importantly, I was afraid for my family, both for their physical and mental health. I was afraid about the impact on my oldest in his first year of high school and for my youngest in a new school for the first time and mostly for my middle son who suffers from anxiety and who I knew would struggle with his own fears.

A hashtag that circulated during the pandemic was #factsnotfear. We make costly decisions when we are afraid. Our survival instinct cuts in and we react instead of pausing to evaluate. We hold dear to our own beliefs even more closely and tightly in an uncertain world. Instead, we need to control our fear of the unknown and seek to validate the facts we come across. We need to consider our truth and the truths of others.

Truth Warriors recognize their own limitations. They rely on the expertise of others and seek information to counter-balance their own beliefs. They push past fear and the need for speed to ensure their decisions are valid. They know that sometimes they need more information and sometimes they need less. This is the dance of seeking truth.

11. The Dance of Seeking Truth

I once worked with a client to enhance accountability within their organization. It was a small business that was "growing up." It had organically grown and changed with the needs of its customers but had now become so big that the style of making decisions and way of getting work done was causing conflict. The business hired us to help define the decision-making process and decision "rights" within the organization.

I started the process with stakeholder interviews, engaging the leaders in the business about what they believed were the challenges and opportunities. As is common in most organizations, there was a clear divide between the VP of Sales and the VP of Operations. The VP of Sales spoke about speed and the fact that competitors were reacting more quickly than ever. He worried that existing processes created a stranglehold on his ability to innovate and react. The VP of Operations highlighted that the desire for speed was creating substantial challenges in her ability to deliver. She saw the processes as being too loose and easily circumvented. Both leaders had the same objective: to deliver product to the customer quickly and profitability.

The culture in this organization was one of intuition. They had been successful by moving quickly with new ideas, without metrics in place to assess the validity of their decisions. They brought innovation to their customers, who saw them as reliable partners. The VP of Operations, new to the company, saw a major gap in how they measured success. She was used to rational decision-making, with key performance indicators (KPIs) in place and business cases to measure the impact of innovation. When she started to measure the performance of the business, she recognized that reliability was starting to slip and new innovation was being delayed due to lack of planning.

We mapped out their current new product development process. In doing so, the VP of Operations pointed out the large number of information gaps. She needed part numbers and supplier quotes and inventory requirements. When we mapped out all the steps required to meet her ideal, we found it took about nine months to launch a new product. We did the same exercise with the VP of Sales. He required much less information, relying on his gut and a few conversations with key customers to tell him that the product would be successful. His new product launch process was estimated to take about three months.

To be successful, these leaders needed to find the balance between their ideals. If they waited to have all the information in place (nine months), they were likely to miss the opportunity to meet an immediate market need. If they pushed too fast (three months), they were likely to run into delivery issues. We worked to map out a process that took about six months, with options to accelerate or slow down based on key metrics built into the process. We created touch points that would allow ongoing validation. Most importantly, we helped both functions to understand the implications of their needs on the other. We encouraged both of them to move to a point somewhere between their default styles.

The dance in truth-seeking is one of balance: knowing when enough information is enough. When your gut or previous experience is valid or when it is leading you down the wrong path. The goal is to be able to move to either end of the spectrum. Those who seek facts must allow themselves to trust their intuition. Those who go with their gut must allow themselves to seek other data or perspectives.

One leader I spoke to shared his perspective on the necessity of this dance. He has his master's degree in engineering and is co-owner of an environmental company specializing in solving water and soil contamination issues. He shared with me that his natural decision style was more rational than intuitive, something that is likely very common for most engineers. As his company grew, he found himself having to make more decisions without all the information he needed. The "engineer in him" wanted all the data but the business leader recognized the need to move forward without. As his career progressed, he found that he moved towards relying more on his intuition. In fact, he recognized that the best decisions were made when he didn't feel 100 percent confident in his decision. He knew that complex decisions involved risk and uncertainty. As he explained, "If you think you are 100 percent certain on a decision, I would almost certainly say you are missing something. You're missing something because nothing is perfect."

I spoke to many leaders about how they navigate complex decisions and each shared the same lessons; they recognized the need to move between intuitive and rational thought and acknowledged a shift in their natural style across the spectrum toward the other end as their career progressed. The goal of the Truth Warrior is to purposefully move within each style as you consider your decisions.

If you are more of rational decision-maker, should you always try to balance that with intuitive thought? Should you purposely try to make every decision without feeling sure that you have all the information? Probably not. But perhaps you should pause when you are feeling lost in the data and ask, "Is this enough? Do I have enough information to trust my gut and move forward?"

If you are more of an intuitive decision-maker, should you always pause to gather more information? Not always. But for more complex decisions or those involving people and change, you will need to allow yourself to pause and consider alternatives. It will be more important than ever to question your beliefs and assumptions and reach out for diverse perspectives.

When decisions tend towards the complex, it is especially important to gather more facts and consider the implications. Complex decisions involve those that are higher risk, encompass more options, or involve the emotions of others. In August 2020, in the midst of the coronavirus pandemic, parents had to make a very complex decision about whether to send their kids back to school in person. In Ontario, the government decided to run normal-sized classrooms for children in kindergarten through grade 8, with those in grade 4 and up required to wear face masks. (Some school boards extended the mandatory mask requirement to the primary grades.) If parents did not feel comfortable sending their kids back, they could opt out and instead rely on a virtual learning system that had experienced numerous problems in the final 3½ months of the previous school year. The decision was to stay home or go back. If parents kept their kids at home, there was a risk to learning and mental health. If parents sent them back, there was a risk to physical health and safety. It was an impossible decision with no easy answer. The data suggested a second outbreak was likely, and indeed a second wave occurred that was worse than the first. Therefore sending them back would be a major risk. Data also suggested death rates in children from COVID-19 were extremely low (in July 2020, one epidemiologist cited a figure of 1 per 10,000 infections). The risk seemed minimal. But when it comes to our children, any risk must be taken seriously. There was no right and wrong in this decision. One can only accept and acknowledge that each family will decide differently—that they will consider the risks and balance rational thought with their intuition.

When decisions tend towards the unknown, a greater degree of intuitive decision-making must happen. We can only rely so much on historical data to shape our future. Historical data is just that: in the past. Leaders who make bold choices need to rely on their instinct. In the 1950s, Bill Allen was the CEO of Boeing. At the time, the company was primarily a defence contractor. Allen proposed the development of a jetliner to take advantage of the growth in civilian air travel and the expected transition from piston-powered to jet-powered airliners. It cost the company $16 million. The Boeing 707 was the result. Tom Ballantyne, a journalist with *Aviator* magazine, described the plane as "not the first jet to enter commercial airline service but … certainly the first to be commercially successful. It dominated air passenger travel through the 1960s and into the 1970s and is generally credited with being the plane that really ushered in the jet age."

Bill Allen took a leap of faith and it paid off. At the time, civilian air travel was still a relatively small industry. This intuitive decision made Boeing a leader in the field. Good leaders recognize the need for both rational and intuitive thought. They might ultimately make a decision based on their intuition, but they will have backed it with contributions from rational thinkers in their group. They will surround themselves with data points and fact checkers and then based on their past and current experience, they will make the decision.

One leader I spoke to shared how he balances rational and intuitive decision-making:

> I've made decisions with no facts, which [cost] millions and millions of dollars, because they were just obviously the right thing to do intuitively. I've made relatively small, hundreds-of-thousands-of-dollars decisions where I've needed facts to make good decisions because of the risk profile or the knock-on impact. I tend to make the decision based on what I think the ripples in the pool are going to look like. And what I mean by that is, if you drop a pebble in a pond, I always try to look beyond the first second or third ripple. That is the basis of whether or not I need to use more rational decision-making or intuitive decision making. It's not a science. I'm sure I get it wrong.

The Truth Warrior is first and foremost a Scout; one who knows that their self-worth is not about being right or wrong. Their ideas are just that—ideas, *not* a reflection of who they are. Their goal is to understand matters using both the facts they uncover and the experience they bring. They know when to pause and consider seeking more information, and when to move forward with the information they have. They are able to say, "Maybe I am wrong about that."

The Truth Warrior is also a Soldier who pushes forward towards an objective, one that is defined by the collective truth of their army. They bring the depth of their experience to any decision but also know when to rely on the tribes that support them. Collectively they are strong; they can set aside the need to win a battle and focus on winning the war.

PART THREE

Speak Truth: Leaning In and Out of Conflict

12. The Conflict Aggressive

I was in mid-career when I transitioned from the back office to the front line. Up until then, I had supporting roles within sales and although I had many direct customer interactions I had never truly "carried the bag." It was never my responsibility to sell directly to the customer. But now I had been promoted to a role where I would manage one of the biggest customers for our business. The company believed in me. I believed in me. Until taking this position, I felt successful in my career.

This role was very different. My past successes did not prepare me. My customer was known to be challenging. My business would be threatened on a regular basis. It was not uncommon for me to get a call that concluded with statements like "If you don't get this to me by the end of the day, I won't run this promotion" or "you will be delisted" or "I will call your manager." The buyer I was dealing with was very conflict-aggressive. He was well-trained and good at intimidating account managers to get what he wanted. I responded in turn—but not to him. Instead, I channelled my aggression inward. I would make demanding requests to my support team, insisting to my supply manager that we would be delisted if we didn't get the product out in time, or telling the marketing manager we would lose listings if they didn't get me promotional material on time.

It came to a head during a particular battle with a peer in the sales strategy group. I was insisting on a promotion that the customer needed. She suggested that it would be off-strategy to do so. Instead of working out a solution that would accommodate both needs, I dug in my heels and fought for my customer. I held strong in my belief that this was the right thing for the business.

In the end, I lost more than the fight for this particular promotion. My manager agreed that running the promotion *was* off-strategy. He told me that I had ruffled feathers in the strategy group and that I was coming across as combative and non-collaborative. He indicated concern that I was struggling in this role and suggested I think about my approach.

For me, it was first and foremost a lesson in humility. I was used to being the expert and relying on myself to drive action. I began to recognize that I didn't have all the answers and that even if I thought I was right, I had to be open to other perspectives. I had been acting out of fear of retribution and allowed my customer to dictate my actions. What was worse, I was using the same stick to beat my team that I was being beaten with.

I continue to be direct in my approach. I am still more aggressive than avoidant when it comes to conflict. I speak more than I listen. I hold strong to beliefs when I should be more open to different perspectives. I recognize this flaw in me and the need to move differently. I know the importance of engaging others, and yet still sometimes struggle to do so.

Truth Warriors who are more aggressive than avoidant need to purposeful about listening to the voices of others. They need to question their own beliefs and instead be open to different perspectives. They need to let go of winning and being right. Instead, they need to focus on the collective truth. They need to work towards less conflict.

13. Why We Need Less Conflict

We need less conflict to stop the divide.

In 2017, the "Mother of All Rallies" was held to support President Trump. Hawk Newsome also attended the rally as the current president of Black Lives Matter's New York chapter. He arrived with half a dozen of other activist prepared to fight against the prevailing beliefs of the stereotypical Trump supporter. They were welcomed with chants like "If you don't like this country, get out." When asked about his expectations for the event, Newsome said, "I expected to come down here and stand here with my fist in the air in a very militant way to exchange insults."

What happened next was a surprise to everyone. While one speaker told the crowd to ignore the protesters and not to "give them the spotlight," Tommy Gunn, one of the event's organizers, took a different path. He invited Hawk up on stage. He told the crowd he was going to let Black Lives Matter speak and "show them what patriotism is all about." He told Newsome, "It's your right to say whatever you believe, and it's their [the crowd's] right to let you know what they think about what you're saying. The important thing is that everybody has a right to speak their mind."

Newsome shared his perspective, often with boos in response from his audience. But he also found commonality. He talked about his own patriotism and his belief in the same God and Bible they all shared. When a man in the audience yelled out "All lives matter!" he agreed, saying "You are right my brother. All lives do matter" before

71

explaining his own position. He ended with a powerful message: "If we really want to make America great, we do it together."

More surprising than the invitation on stage was the connection that occurred after his speech. Trump supporters approached Newsome to show support for him. One of the heads of Bikers for Trump asked to take a picture of Newsome and the biker's son. "Here I went from being the enemy to someone they want to take pictures with their children," Newsome later said. "That's the power of communication."

Newsome himself also gained a new perspective on the Trump supporters he was showing up to fight. In an interview after the event he said:

> It kind of restored some of my faith in these people because when I spoke truths, they agreed. I feel like two sides that never listen to each other, actually made progress today. If not on a grander level, but just person to person, I think we really made some substantial steps without either side yielding anything.

I showcase this story not to advocate for less protest but to support the need for thoughtful disagreement. There is a need to call for change, but to truly enable change, we must also be willing to listen to the voices of others. Newsome recognized that neither party gave anything up but instead had a better understanding of one another.

This issue surfaced again in 2020 in response to the death of George Floyd at the hands of a Minneapolis police officer. Many of you have likely seen the chilling video. His death evoked a strong reaction from black communities across the world in what I hope will be a tipping point for greater racial equality. What is happening now is both a convergence and diversion of opinions and beliefs.

Black Lives Matter was founded in 2013 with the mission of eradicating white supremacy and building local power to intervene in violence inflicted on Black communities by the state and vigilantes. Before Floyd's death, this movement played an active role in protesting other injustices, but the message was primarily heard by the Black community. As at the 2017 Trump rally, other groups would counter with the statement "All lives matter," one which rang true for a lot of people, causing them to ignore the more pressing message of "Black lives matter."

As a white woman, I can acknowledge that it took me time to understand the nature of the "Black lives matter vs. all lives matter" discussion. When a white person heard the phrase "Black lives matter," it sounded a bit like "your life doesn't matter." That was never the intention of the message but it incited anger. In 2020, Black Lives Matter hit a tipping point with broader communities finally starting to see the message as a cry for help and change rather than as challenge to their own existence.

Social media has helped to communicate this message. When I paid attention and sought out information, I found many great examples that explained the concept. One is of a dinner party where Bob says, "I am hungry," and his fellow tablemates respond, "Everyone is hungry, Bob." Bob adds, "But I don't have any food on my plate." Once again the response is "Everyone is hungry, Bob" and the group begins to eat. The statement "everyone is hungry" is accurate but it does not address the need expressed by Bob. Saying "all lives matter" when someone else says "Black lives matter" is ignoring this need. It's the same when I say "breast cancer is bad"; that does not mean other cancers are not bad. The two statements are not mutually exclusive. I needed to listen before I truly heard this message.

> **We need less conflict to listen to other perspectives.**

Being less conflict aggressive means being willing to listen to the other side. It means recognizing that your opinion is a mere reflection of your current beliefs. We cannot assume our own ideas are true. Leaders in business tend to have a strong voice but also must systematically allow for the voice of others. They must be humble in their belief that their voice is not the only voice. They need to listen to other perspectives.

In 1975, Ray Dalio started Bridgewater, an asset management firm, out of his apartment. Within a few years he opened an office and had some initial successes with accurate market predictions. His opinions were strong and although built on rational models, were sometimes wrong. Predictions of the future often are. The challenge for Dalio early in his business was that he was so confident in his own perspective, and so unwilling to consider other alternatives, that he put everything at risk.

In 1982, Dalio predicted that the economy would fall into a deep recession. His perspective was controversial. He invested his money and his clients' money accordingly. Instead of declining as predicted, the stock market rose and continued to do so for the next 18 years. Ray lost everything. He had to let go every one of his employees and had to borrow money from his father to get by. He was at a crossroads and had to decide whether to continue to pursue his dream or to move back towards a corporate role. He chose the former and Bridgewater Associates as of October 2017 was worth over $160 billion. He acknowledges that this failure was one of life's greatest lessons.

In his book *Principles* and the video *Principles for Success by Ray Dalio*, he shares the learnings from that event. Although there are many, my key takeaway was his acknowledgement of the need to think differently. He believed:

> To succeed, we must embrace all our realities, especially the harsh realities that we wish weren't true. At first, looking at these harsh realities caused me a lot of pain. But I learned that this pain was just psychological, and that my seeing things differently made all the difference.

> Ray Dalio began to recognize that he did not have all the answers.

> My big mistake in betting on a depression gave me a healthy fear of being wrong. In other words, it gave me deep humility, which was exactly what I needed. To succeed, I needed to see more than I alone could see.

He knew that in order to expand what he could see, he had to stop focusing on being right and start focusing on what is true. He purposely sought out people who disagreed with him:

> To get it, I needed to replace the joy of being proven right with the joy of learning what's true. This need prompted me

to seek out the most thoughtful people I could find who disagreed with me. I didn't care about their conclusions, I just wanted to see things through their eyes, and to have them see things through my eyes, so that together we could hash things out to discover what's true.

Those who are conflict assertive tend to have strong opinions. Instead, they need humility and a recognition that their view may not be the correct one. To be beneficial, conflict needs to be constructive and productive. It can't be personal. I spoke to a professor who teaches a course on human rights about her perspective on conflict. She has difficult conversations with her students on big topics from Indigenous issues to genocide. She sees conflict play out in her classroom. She explained the reason we sometimes struggle with it:

> We don't train people how to be constructive in their conflict. Instead, we are defensive and we are aggressive and we're disrespectful and we're hateful or this or that, and we think everything is so polarized. It's like, if I don't agree with you, I hate you.

Truth Warriors understand the importance of humility. They recognize that conflict can only be beneficial if they are open to the beliefs and ideas of others. They know that the best decisions are made by respecting diverse opinions and creating harmony and positive tension. Those who are conflict aggressive need to remember to listen to others and work towards finding commonality where division exists. Those who are conflict avoidant have a different challenge.

14. The Conflict Avoidant

Carrie was a former colleague of mine who established a small networking group for up-and-coming female entrepreneurs. It included only eight women as regular participants, meeting every six weeks to discuss our common challenges. A few years back Carrie struggled personally and professionally. Her attendance at our meetings began to decline. We understood. As the meeting approached, she would confirm her attendance, even sometimes up to the hour before. However, she never did show up. Rather than share with us the fact that she needed some time to regroup and sort through her life, she continued to tell us she planned to attend, although she never would. The implication of this behaviour is that we lost trust in her assertions. She would email to say "I'll see you tomorrow" when all of us knew that we would not.

Fast forward two years later. Carrie is running a successful small business but does not speak to the group members. After almost a year of saying she would attend and then not showing up, she stopped making the declaration. She completely removed herself from the group that she created without a reason why. We no longer believed that she would attend and my guess is that despite having gotten sorted out, she is too embarrassed to return after neglecting us for so long. We would happily have her back and we would have happily supported her through her sabbatical.

I can only guess that it was too difficult for Carrie to speak up to tell us the reason for her departure. For us, it felt like a betrayal because we would have understood her need to step away from the group. We would have supported her. Her inability to ask for that support felt like a lack of trust in us. At the same time, we lost trust in her. Trust that she would attend as she had committed to do. When we avoid difficult conversations, we erode trust and degrade relationships.

For Carrie, keeping quiet was the path of least resistance. It was easier for her to avoid us altogether than to be vulnerable and forthright. The Scout's role in battle is to speak up, even if doing so is unpleasant. Unpleasantness is something we naturally want to avoid. When something is difficult to say, we want to avoid it. Most of us dislike conflict. We want to be liked. We want to avoid hurting those we care about. We are told "If you don't have anything nice to say, don't say anything at all". Leaning in to conflict means not taking the path of least resistance. Sometimes this stops us from challenging decisions when we should.

Truth Warriors who are more avoidant than aggressive need to be purposeful about sharing their voice. They need to recognize the importance of their message, even when unpleasant. They know how to create harmony. They need to remember to also create tension. In doing so, they allow for debate and enable better decisions. Sometimes they need more conflict.

15. Why We Need More Conflict

We need more conflict to advocate for others.

In early 2017, my husband began experiencing massive headaches. It became so unbearable that the only relief was the need to lie down, immediately. We spent Easter weekend in the hospital waiting for his first MRI. We left the hospital that weekend with an answer: he had a cerebrospinal fluid (CSF) leak. This meant that somewhere in the dura mater—the outermost layer of connective tissue that surrounds the brain and spinal cord, and which keeps the fluid from escaping—there was an opening that was allowing the CSF to escape and his brain to sag. The good news (if you could call it that) was that we now knew the cause of his headaches. The bad news was the doctors didn't know where the leak was. It could be anywhere in the brain or spinal cord. Such leaks are most commonly caused by epidurals accidently puncturing the dura mater. The preferred solution for a CSF leak is what's called a blood patch. Essentially, they inject your own blood into the dura mater, hoping it finds the hole and seals it. For a small hole (like an epidural nick) this is normally effective. It was not for my husband.

So began the need for more blood patches and more tests. Lying down was a short-term cure, primarily because it allowed the reservoir of fluid around the brain to fill back up. We were in and out of hospitals, often a few days at a time. The thinking was that eventually the blood patch would "take" and he would be fine. He required bed rest in between.

What the doctors didn't know was that this was not a small pin-prick of a hole. This was a gaping hole made larger by a herniated disc that was poking in to the dura mater. Unfortunately, the way we found this out was quite traumatic. At some point, lying down was not enough and Mike began to feel more and more unwell even when he wasn't standing up. Early one morning he woke me up and told me had to go to the hospital now. I took him and we spent the normal amount of timing encouraging the folks at triage to please let him lie down. We knew what he had.

This was our third hospital visit. I knew the lay of the land now. I asked the nurses for Gravol to calm his stomach. All seemed relatively normal, although Mike seemed slightly more out of it than usual. I blamed it on the Gravol. When dinner time came, he asked me to bring a slice of pizza up to the room for him. We shared the meal together. As we chatted, he told me about a conversation he had with his mother while I was getting the pizza. I thought it was odd that she had called at that time but didn't think much more about it. We were waiting on an MRI scheduled for the morning. The next day I had an early morning meeting and wouldn't get back to him until around 10 a.m. Since hospital schedules are always subject to change, I asked my stepmother to be there with Mike at 8 a.m. in case the MRI took place early. I kissed him good night and told him I would see him in the morning and to text me if he heard anything more about the timing of the test. On the way home I called his parents about their phone call. They hadn't spoken to him. I told them that it was worrisome if his memory was being affected and that I'd have to keep an eye on it.

When I woke up I hadn't heard from Mike. I assumed he was still asleep. As I walked into my meeting (a 45-minute drive from the hospital), my stepmother called me. She had arrived at 8 a.m. but Mike had already been sent for the MRI. I thought that was odd since he hadn't let me know. I had time to wait before my meeting so I asked her to have him call me when he got back to the room. She called back 10 minutes later. I asked her why he didn't call and she told me that he did not know how to operate the phone. "What do you mean he doesn't know how to use the phone?" I responded. In hindsight, I realize that she wasn't aware of the condition I had left him in the night before. The man I spoke to the night before was coherent, perhaps a little confused and drowsy but otherwise completely normal. The man in the hospital that morning was incoherent, unable to speak or do even simple tasks. His brain was bleeding.

All of this I still did not fully understand until later. I only knew that something was off. I asked her to call me if his condition worsened and that I would get through my meeting as quickly as possible. When I left that meeting 45 minutes later, I called her. She told me that Mike was being transferred to another hospital that specialized in neurology and that he was being prepped for brain surgery. The drive to that hospital was the longest of my life. I needed to get there before he went in.

I made it. In "hospital hours," "prepping for surgery" apparently takes quite a few. I sat with him for two hours before they took him away. It was during that time that I learned that his brain had sagged so substantially from lack of fluid that it hemorrhaged and was bleeding. The surgery was intended to reduce the pressure. The man before me was unrecognizable. He muttered gibberish. He did not know who I was or where he was. If he did not recover, he would be left with severe brain damage. He was 45 years old.

While I was waiting for his surgery, the heart monitor strapped to him continued to beep. As anyone who has sat by a loved one in the hospital can attest, the sound of the alarms on those monitors is the most bone-chilling sound you can hear. It signalled that his heart rate was dropping. He was in a room where he was being monitored. One station for two rooms. I called out to the attendant. "His heart rate is dropping." She told me she knew and that the doctor was aware of the situation. For two hours this went on. I didn't feel confident enough to speak up against the experts who were monitoring him. I could only trust that they knew more than I did.

Eventually the doctor came. When he did, it was clear that he was not as aware of the situation as the attendant had indicated. He looked alarmed. So alarmed in fact that he asked the support staff to "take this man to surgery now." I was signing authorization papers as they wheeled him away. I chased them down the hall and he evacuated the elevator to get him in to the operating room as fast as possible. I had not advocated for him enough. I did not speak up when I should have. His life was at risk because I had not pushed that attendant harder.

When Mike recovered from his brain surgery, we still had the underlying problem to solve. The leak had not been fixed and now its implications were greater. He had to stay in bed until they could find a solution. The first step was to get him to a specialist to see if the leak's location could be isolated. This itself took time, and although I tried to advocate for the process to move faster, it was beyond my control.

I had many more opportunities to advocate for my husband during his stay in the hospital. After brain surgery at the second hospital we were in waiting mode. But we made progress. We went to a specialist in Toronto who was able to identify the source of the leak, which was located in his upper spine. A herniated disc was continuing to puncture the dura mater and re-create a hole. This hole was not about to be easily patched. It would require spinal surgery to remove the disc and sew the hole up. They would need to go in through Mike's back, break through his ribs, and cut through the dura to the other side to be able to patch the hole, which was actually at the front of his body. It was horrific news but at least we felt like we had a solution. Except that we didn't. As it turns out, there are few surgeons in Canada who perform this type of surgery. The only expert currently identified as willing to do such surgery was a surgeon in Los Angeles who specialized in CSF leaks. By this point, I had become quite an expert on the subject. I had joined a Facebook group for others with the same condition and learned that many were in the same boat—waiting for someone to fix the leak and confined to their beds (or at least close to one) in order to control the pain associated with the condition. Matters felt bleak and again we waited.

We were told that the next step would be to see a radiologist at the hospital where the specialist first discovered the location of the leak. They would advise if we could be referred on to the LA surgeon. As we waited, Mike's birthday came. His condition seemed relatively stable. The doctors agreed to let him leave his hospital bed for a few hours with his family to go out for dinner. He did and we appreciated the opportunity to see him in a normal situation.

Unfortunately, a few days later Mike experienced new symptoms. He lost sensation in one of his arms. He could no longer lift it or move his fingers. At the same time this was happening, the hospital was looking at releasing him to go home in order to free up a hospital bed. This was my opportunity to advocate again. I tracked down the surgeon who did the brain surgery. We were lucky if we saw him once a day and relied on him as our primary care contact. He would be the one to write the order to release Mike. When he arrived at the room, I asked him why we aren't being more proactive about a solution. Why are we waiting while my husband continued to experience potentially dangerous symptoms? This was his first awareness of the symptoms and he took them seriously, but he also responded in what I was learning was a typical way in our health-care system. He told us that the hand numbness was possibly the result of a further brain bleed, and that Mike would be kept in the hospital on full bed rest and monitored. If he needed another operation to reduce the pressure in his brain, they could do that. I was no longer willing to be quiet. "Why are we not finding the solution to the leak instead of waiting for his brain to bleed?" I asked. At this point, both Mike and I were emotionally drained. He had been in and out of hospitals for three months as doctors sought to understand his situation. His condition was deteriorating and now he would be confined to bed to prevent further possible brain damage. We knew the problem and we knew the solution, but we didn't know the path to get there. I told the doctor that we couldn't just sit here and wait and hope that he didn't need another surgery before the operation that would save him. The next day we were told that we would be going to Toronto Western, one of the top neurological hospitals in Canada.

In true hospital fashion, we didn't know exactly why. We thought it was to see the radiologist who would then put us on the path to LA. As it turns out, the doctor I spoke to at the second hospital had made a call to a surgeon at Toronto Western and convinced him to do the surgery. The doctor in question had carried out many spinal surgeries before but none for this purpose. Again, I had to speak up. I had to ask anyone who would listen why we were there until we got the answer. The surgeon met with us and explained that he would be doing the surgery.

We had a path and we had a plan. It was a relief. But there were still times when I needed to speak up for Mike. On day two of his hospital stay, I arrived to find the order "NPO." I had to start by finding out what that meant. It turned out it means "nothing by mouth"—no food or drink. I then had to find out why that was happening. Unfortunately for Mike, he was bedridden and didn't have the luxury I had of wandering the hospital halls to find someone who could answer questions. One person told me that Mike was given that order because he might go into surgery that day. This was news to us. The surgeon we saw the day before had suggested that it would be later in the week. We were both happy and nervous about this news. So now I was on a new quest to find out if he was *actually* having surgery that day. I finally tracked down a resident who had been assigned to Mike's case. I asked him why Mike wasn't allowed to eat. He confirmed that it was because surgery was a possibility. I then asked him how likely it was that Mike would go in to surgery that day. His answer: "I'd say there is a zero percent chance." I am fairly strong in math, and I guessed that as a doctor he was too, so I confirmed what he just said: "So, he will not be going in to surgery today?" He answered "No," and I asked: "So can he eat? Because it's now almost lunch time and he has eaten nothing all day." The doctor replied, "I think so but let me check." Forty-five minutes later Mike was allowed to eat. Had I not been there to advocate for him, it is entirely possible that he wouldn't have eaten for most of the day.

He had the surgery at the end of that week. It was eight long hours of waiting. We had been warned that aside from death (which is a risk in every surgery), there was also a risk of complete paralysis or temporary paralysis, given that they were operating on his spine. My husband, the complete non-risk-taker, knew that there was no other choice. It was either the surgery or confinement to a bed for the rest of his life. When he first woke up, he could move his toes. A few days later Mike was walking. One week later he was able to come home.

Before all was said and done, I had to advocate for Mike one last, crucial time. After his surgery, his breathing was irregular. His monitor continued to sound the alarm to indicate his oxygen levels. The scene felt eerily familiar. Unfortunately for Mike, the medications he had been given to control the pain were impacting his breathing. Every time he drifted off to sleep, the alarm would sound. And every time, I would run to the station to tell them. I was not about to let anyone tell me that "he is okay. We are monitoring him." I was not about to watch my husband deteriorate without speaking up. The doctors and nurses ultimately saved his life but I believe that had I not been willing to speak up on his behalf when he wasn't able, the outcome may not have been the same.

This situation was life and death. But we deal with the opportunity to speak up or be silent every day. I struggled to speak up for my husband at the start of our journey because I did not feel it was my place. I was not the expert. Often times, we avoid conflict because we don't believe our opinion is valid. We allow our inner critic to convince us that our ideas are wrong or that someone must know better. This is the biggest risk in staying silent in decision making. A counter-view of a situation or outcome is necessary to validate our decisions. It is only by sharing our unique perspective that we can be certain the people around us are considering the right alternatives. Everybody deserves to believe that they are good enough; that their opinion is worthwhile. If we shy away from confrontational conversations, we don't allow ourselves the opportunity to express our ideas. Conflict is necessary to ultimately reduce conflict and build trust. It allows us to challenge wrong decisions.

> **We need more conflict to challenge wrong decisions.**

I was 13 years old when I watched with anticipation as the first teacher was about to launch into space aboard the space shuttle *Challenger*. I watched in horror 73 seconds later when the shuttle exploded, killing all seven crew members. The actual technical failure was later found to involve so-called "O-rings" designed to seal the joints between the segments of the solid-rocket boosters that helped propel the shuttle into orbit. Under extremely cold conditions like those on the fateful day of *Challenger*'s launch, the O-ring did not position itself in its groove properly because it was too stiff and brittle. As a result, the booster seal burnt through, releasing a super-hot plume of gas that ultimately cut through the hardware attaching the booster to the vehicle as well as rupturing the giant external tank filled with liquid hydrogen and liquid oxygen. This was the immediate cause of the accident, but later a special commission appointed to investigate the loss of the *Challenger* determined that NASA's flawed organizational culture and decision-making processes had been key contributing factors to the accident.

It was a known fact that there was a risk of the O-rings failing at low temperatures. It was also known on the morning of the launch that the external temperature (well below freezing during the previous night) wasn't high enough to meet launch requirements. The night before the launch, Bob Ebeling, one of the engineers working for contractor Morton Thiokol, which built the solid-rocket boosters, told his wife that he believed *Challenger* would blow up. NASA managers and Morton Thiokol executives chose to disregard warnings from concerned engineers about the danger. Ebling openly wept when his prediction came true.

For the years prior to the launch, interest in space travel had been in decline. The excitement of the moon landing was far in the past, and space travel was coming to be viewed as routine. The *Challenger* mission was intended to change all that. It was the first mission to launch a civilian into space and was expected to pave the way for further such flights. As a result, the launch became very public. Schools were expected to watch it live as the first teacher travelled into space.

The management team at NASA was also excited by the mission and under pressure to deliver it. More importantly, they believed in it and believed it was their job to make it happen. Jesse W. Moore, NASA's associate administrator of human space flight and the executive responsible for the shuttle program, had been named director of the Johnson Space Center just five days before the accident. The *Challenger* launch, initially set for July 1985, had already been delayed several times—first to December 1985 and then to January 1986. Technical problems and then bad weather forced further postponements. There were political reasons why Tuesday needed to be the day. The State of the Union address was scheduled for that night, and U.S. President Ronald Reagan planned to talk about the space program. Christa McAuliffe, the successful "Teacher in Space" candidate, was planning a live broadcast on the fourth day in space. If the launch was delayed again, that day of the mission would be a Saturday, making the televised lesson impossible. Both Reagan's speech and McAuliffe's lesson were opportunities for NASA to generate publicity and support for the shuttle program, which was much needed at the time. Scrubbing the Tuesday launch would rob them of this opportunity.

The senior management team who sat in a room prior to launch and decided the fate of the *Challenger* did not have all the information, nor did they want it. They believed they were taking an acceptable risk. The shuttle had launched and returned safely to earth 24 times before. No one in the room wanted to challenge what was their common desire: to have a successful mission. NASA managers insulated Jesse Moore from the debate over the integrity of the rocket booster seals. After the explosion, he stated: "All of the people involved in this program, to my knowledge, felt that Challenger was quite ready to go. And I made the decision, along with the recommendations from the teams supporting me, that we launch."

Although alarms were sounded, the desire to carry on with the mission took precedence. Senior managers who did know of the O-ring problems did not speak up, not necessarily because they were afraid of repercussions, but because they supported one another. Their shared belief and commitment to the same goal stopped them from seeking out and paying attention to crucial information that would argue against launch that morning. They cohesively pushed forward toward their goal only to see matters end in disaster.

"The opposite of courage is not cowardice, it is conformity. Even a dead fish can go with the flow." —Jim Hightower

The *Challenger* launch decision is used today as a perfect example of "groupthink": when the desire for harmony or conformity results in an irrational or dysfunctional outcome. It teaches us that conflict avoidance can lead to catastrophic outcomes. There can also be implications for individuals and teams who avoid conflict. Although sometimes, we avoid conflict due to fear, many times the desire for unity is what stops us from challenging the status quo. Instead, we need conflict to challenge group decisions and test assumptions.

We need more conflict to test our own assumptions.

A few years back, I worked with a sales and marketing team. The leader invited me in because she believed there was tension among the members. In talking with each of them individually, I quickly understood her concern. It was clear that the team valued harmony. Relationships and collaboration were a key priority. More than once I heard people say things like "I really want to work better with [insert name here] but I don't think he's listening." There was a desire for connection but also a belief that the other members "just don't get me." I was dealing with a group of conflict-avoidant individuals who did not want to hurt one another or "rock the boat" but also felt that their concerns were not being validated.

Julie, a key account manager, talked about her relationship with Tim, a trade marketing manager. Their job was to work together to bring new solutions to the customer. Julie informed me that Tim was so focused on the launch plan for their new product that he didn't understand the needs of her customer. He never asked her about what she needed. When I spoke to Tim, he told me he struggled with Julie because she doesn't seem to want to provide any feedback about how her customer might react whenever he spoke about the new product. Both in fact had the same goal—an effective launch—but neither felt understood.

When I understood the challenge, I asked Julie how she had informed Tim about her concern. She paused. She told me that Tim had asked for feedback about the launch and she sent him information about her customer. He hadn't acknowledged it. He didn't seem interested. She believed he was so focused on getting the product out that implications for her customer didn't matter. I asked her how she knew he wasn't interested. She paused again. Tim had never directly stated that the information wasn't useful and Julie had never asked him if that was the case. She had assumed it to be true because of his lack of reaction. She also had never directly spoken to him about her feelings about being ignored when she was trying to help.

I asked Tim about the information he got from Julie. He told me that it had provided some good context but he didn't understand how it linked to the product launch. He believed that Julie was hiding something that might be relevant. I asked him to tell me some of the questions he asked Julie to help clarify relevance. He paused. He hadn't asked her about it. He assumed she didn't want to provide feedback. Other account managers provided a lot more detail while Julie just didn't seem to care about this launch. He needed to focus on customers who would support it. I asked him how he knew that Julie didn't care about the launch. He paused again. He didn't. He had assumed because of the information provided that Julie was uninterested. Tim did not follow up with her or share his concern that she didn't seem to care about his work.

Julies and Tims can be found in every team and in every organization in some form. It is easy to jump to conclusions about the intentions of others. In this case, both Julie and Tim had the same goal. They also had the same desire to be collaborative. Yet neither felt heard nor understood. Both had a role to play in testing their assumptions. Instead, they became resentful and withdrawn and the team's performance suffered.

Conflict avoidance can have many negative outcomes. It can stop us from advocating for ourselves and others. It can remove an important voice from the table. It can make us resent others. In decision-making, all voices are essential. One CEO I spoke with articulated this idea best. "I'm supportive of what I call constructive tension," she said. "I want that push and pull. I actually don't think the best decision is ever realized, without having some level of discourse or differences in opinion."

Truth Warriors recognize the common desire for peace can only achieved through battle—positive, respectful, change-educing battle. Truth Warriors encourage tension. They advocate for others and allow one another to express differences. They insist upon it. They recognize that conflict doesn't need to be a dirty word. Instead, they recognize that sometimes they need more conflict and sometimes they need less. This is the dance of speaking truth.

—

16. The Dance of Speaking Truth

My husband and I fall on different sides of the conflict spectrum. I am the type of person that needs to "get it all out." I want to share my thoughts. I want you to share yours. When we are fighting, I want all the cards on the table. I want respectful, honest dialogue and I want it sooner rather than later. My husband falls more towards the conflict-averse side of the spectrum. He is naturally more collaborative then I am. He prefers space and introspection to figure things out before he engages in discussion.

When stress comes into our lives, I become more conflict aggressive, making snide comments to him to express my discontent. He becomes more conflict averse, hiding out in the basement and less likely to engage in conversation. While Mike pulls away to calm the storm, I am building up all the arguments for why I am right. I am not giving it space. I am allowing it to build. I am fuelling the fire. When the conflict comes to a head, I have a day's worth of thoughts about why he was wrong. In turn, this sends his conflict aversion into high gear and he retreats.

We came to recognize the flaw in this cycle of behaviour. First, we had to recognize that the way we handled conflict was different. I had to allow Mike the space to escape and he had to try to come out sooner. I also had to recognize my own desire to be right when conflict did come up. The lesson for me was to acknowledge my own tendencies. I couldn't stop the internal argument that was going on in my mind. I had an answer for every "fact" someone threw at me. Whether I was asking for advice, or trying to settle an argument, I felt like I had the right answer. The trick was to convince myself that maybe I didn't.

Mike explained to me that many times it felt like I was "selling my ideas to him" rather than truly understanding his position. My background is in sales and analytics and, as a consultant, I need to sell my ideas all the time. That is my full-time job. I would not be successful in my career if I didn't have that skill. However, selling ideas instead of listening or engaging was putting my relationship at risk. Mike and I agreed on a cue to help me through this. When I got into this selling mode with my husband, he would say, "You're selling me right now." It made me pause. It made me consider my words. It would help me to recognize that I should be leaning out of conflict instead of leaning in.

Ray Dalio also learned the dance of speaking truth. He learned to consider other perspectives and be less conflict aggressive. He also recognized the need to avoid being conflict averse. At Bridgewater, he has created a culture built on the belief that it is important to acknowledge what you don't know; to allow yourself to be wrong but also embrace what he calls "radical transparency." In an interview he explained the purpose of this, saying that he believed

> the greatest tragedy of mankind is that people have ideas and opinions in their heads but don't have a process for properly examining these ideas to find out what's true. That creates a world of distortions. That's relevant to what we do, and I think it's relevant to all decision making. So when I say I believe in radical truth and radical transparency, all I mean is we take things that ordinary people would hide, and we put them on the table, particularly mistakes, problems, and weaknesses.

When we speak truth, we understand the dance. We may not always execute it flawlessly, but we recognize the need to move within conflict. The Truth Warrior is both Scout and Soldier and knows when and how to play each role. Complex decisions require the need to allow for thoughtful disagreement and active listening. We must recognize the differences in others and the natural tendencies in ourselves. To be successful, it starts with understanding the Warrior within us.

PART FOUR

The Warrior Within Us

17. Understanding Your Decision and Conflict Style

The Scout in battle is one who seeks truth and pauses to understand. The Soldier in battle moves forward towards a common goal, knowing when to strike and when to retreat. It is this delicate dance within the battle that will win the war. Truth Warriors understand this dance. It is one of fluidity of movement, of individual expression and group interconnection. It can be fast-paced or slow moving, inwards or outwards, powerful or gentle. The movements are intentional. The Truth Warrior must also move in this way.

It starts with understanding where you are. Bias shapes our beliefs and behaviours but we are also impacted by our natural tendencies. We each will lean towards rational or intuitive decision-making. We each have a natural preference to avoid or engage in difficult conversations. These are shaped by our past experiences but can also develop over time. These are not static personality traits but are opportunities to move another way. They are opportunities to dance.

The intersection of how you make decisions and how you embrace conflict will affect your ability to navigate complex decisions. The interconnection of these concepts is illustrated in the model that you'll find on the next page.

The further you are to either end of the two axes, the bigger the opportunity for you to learn to move the other way. Truth Warriors fall in the middle and allow themselves to move back and forth across the spectrum depending on the situation and the individuals they are interacting with. Tribes of Truth Warriors should include a diverse spectrum of individuals to help balance out how they engage.

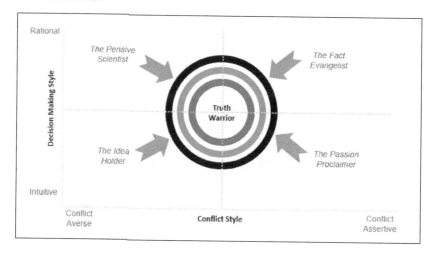

Armies or organizations that have too many people in any one quadrant will want to think about how this imbalance affects their ability to make effective decisions.

I have developed an assessment to help you understand your natural tendencies in two areas: decision styles and conflict styles. The measure of rational vs. intuitive was adapted from the Rational-Experiential Inventory created in 1996 by Epstein, Pacini, Denes-Raj, and Heier. The measure of conflict was adapted from the Rathus Assertiveness Schedule (RAS) created by Spencer Rathus in 1973 as well as the TLK model of conflict. These are tools that are considered valid assessments by the research community although like any scientific finding, the results continue to be challenged.

Before you read on, to find out more about your natural tendencies you can take the assessment on my website. The result will plot you on this matrix across both spectra. You might find that you are highly rational but in the middle of the conflict spectrum. Or you might find yourself to be very conflict assertive but in the middle in terms of your rational/intuitive preferences.

These findings are not meant to be labels or an evaluation of your personality. They are opportunities to increase awareness of our natural tendencies and the strengths and risks associated with each. In the next sections, I will talk about how each assessment can offer value to an organization and also discuss considerations for those who fall into each quadrant and how to work with them. People don't fit into buckets and you may find that some of these descriptions resonate more with you then others. That is okay. My primary goal in this assessment is to have you reflect on how you make decisions and feel about conflict, as well as consider how others do these things.

The next few chapters will explain each of these styles in detail. Although you should find benefits in reviewing your own, it will also help you to read through those of others. In particular, each section contains "Tips for your dance partners" which will explain how to best engage with these types of decisions makers. In addition, you may find that you are within a culture or operating on a team that is different from your typical decision style. This is an important insight as it will allow you to shift your approach and better understand who you are working with. This will help you to move differently.

18. The Pensive Scientist

Elaine works as a sales analyst at a company that produces flooring. She started in the role six months ago, having done similar work at her previous company. This position was a step up for her, providing her with greater responsibility to build analytic capability in the organization. It was also a new role in the company. It was Elaine's job to forecast next month's production by product group. Previously this would have been done by the finance team, a process which produced inconsistent results. Her goal was to be more accurate in her predictions.

After spending a few months getting up to speed, her first opportunity to influence the sales forecast arrived. As in her prior role, Elaine used historical data in combination with some assumptions to model her prediction. Given it was her first time making the forecast, she wanted to be accurate and detailed. She began work two weeks prior to submission and was required to submit her projection on the Monday before a planned Friday meeting. She re-did the model multiple times, adjusting the assumptions each time until she felt confident. She worked late Sunday night to complete her model, put everything in a PowerPoint deck and sent it to the Finance Director, who would integrate the forecast into the monthly operations meeting.

A few days later she sat at the meeting, excited to see the results of her work. She predicted a reasonable growth rate of 3 percent and had provided multiple facts to support the rationale behind her prediction. When the finance director addressed next month's forecast, he put up an expected growth rate of 7 percent and then moved on to the next chart. There was no basis for his prediction, and he didn't show any of the work she had put together. As the meeting was winding down, he asked if there were any questions. Elaine did not want to be confrontational, so she remained quiet. Later she asked her manager, who also attended the meeting, why the number had changed. She was told that her prediction was too conservative. Elaine left feeling resentful for the amount of work she put in and confused about her role in the company. She wondered whether she had what it took to do her job.

Elaine is both a rational decision-maker and conflict adverse. Her typical style is the "Pensive Scientist." These individuals typically make well-thought-out decisions and are fact-based in their thinking but struggle to share those facts or may back down easily when someone asks them to defend their thinking.

These individuals tend to take more time to make decisions. In Elaine's case, she went back and forth multiple times and worked right up to the deadline before she felt confident. The risk for this style is feeling that you need to have all the information before you can move forward. The other challenge is the ability of others to see the data as you do. A rational mind may see patterns others do not. The details are important to such individuals, but they may not showcase the resulting message in simple terms. When challenged or ignored, these individuals struggle to push back and reinforce their findings.

Benefits of this Style
- Your decisions are well thought-out.
- You enhance team harmony in decision making.
- You help others to validate and think through decisions.

Risks of this Style
- You may take too much time to make decisions.
- The team may not understand your thought process or get lost in too many facts.
- You may remain quiet even when you disagree with decisions.

Learning Some New Dance Moves
If your style is the Pensive Scientist, consider the following opportunities to enhance your impact and move into conflict and towards intuitive decision-making:

- Allow yourself to make decisions without all the information. Trust your instincts.
- Shift your message away from the data and towards the desired outcome.
- Find opportunities to express yourself, even if in writing or one-on-one conversations.

Dance Tips for Your Partners

If you are working with others who are Pensive Scientists, consider the following to effectively engage them in your decision process:

- Give them time to gather and disseminate data.
- Allow them to be the validator for your decisions. Ask for data that counteracts your belief. These folks will find it if it's there.
- Enable them to use different forms of communication. They may not feel comfortable sharing in a group setting.

Leading a Tribe of Pensive Scientists

If your team is made up primarily of such individuals, you will want to think about the implications for decision-making. Collectively this group can get lost in facts and the need to find more data. They may ask one another lots of questions that stray away from the key problem. They may delay important decisions because they feel they don't have enough information to move forward. To help this tribe:

- Allow this group to be thorough in their decision process but also be clear about deadlines. You will benefit from the quality and depth of their output.
- Define the problem up front and refer back to it during the process to stay on track. Re-direct if the facts they are presenting are leading them away from the core objective.
- Align on the framework for sharing recommendations. Test for simplicity and relevance in their final outputs.

An Army of Pensive Scientists

Cultures that embody this style are typically those based in science or which have a complex solution that is difficult to convey. They understand what they are offering, but they may struggle to sell it. They may take longer to get to products to market because they do a lot of research on the likelihood of success.

I worked with a client that sold nutritional products that were heavily grounded in scientific research. They sold into the medical community and to retailers. They had been successful because of their ability to understand the data behind their product and to speak the language of the medical community they were influencing. When they moved their focus beyond the medical community towards consumer communication and retailer support, they struggled.

The product was highly effective and the messaging behind the brand was strong, but they could not make it succinct or digestible. Their portfolio was complex, and differences between products were not clear. In addition, the sales and marketing team, often from the medical field themselves, wrote copy that focused on scientific benefits instead of user benefits. To succeed, they had to simplify. They had to let go of trying to explain everything.

We started by clarifying their offer. I worked with many different stakeholders, asking them to articulate the benefits of their products. Each time they went down the rabbit hole of focusing on the health benefits of each ingredient ("Glucosamine is great for joint care!"), I encouraged them to think "up" a level. Why do I need joint care? "To improve mobility." Why do I want to improve mobility? "So I can do the things I love." That last sentence stated the benefit with no scientific evidence, but it was much more likely to resonate with consumers than "Glucosamine is great for joint care" ever would.

Cultures of Pensive Scientists need to challenge themselves to let go of detail and hone in on audience requirements. They need to engage in "lay" conversations regularly to test that their messaging resonates with others, particularly non-specialists. They need to become more comfortable with conflict, recognizing their voice as an important contribution.

19. The Fact Evangelist

Tracy is an engineer who was promoted up the ranks to become a plant manager at a company that manufactures hand sanitizer. She was asked to put together a proposal for capital spend on new equipment to increase output. She had a week to plan her presentation for Jada, the VP of Operations, who would decide whether it was a worthwhile investment. In preparation, Tracy gathered facts on the current yield rates for the line and the predicted yield rates with the new equipment. She estimated the payback period would be three years.

When the day came to share her recommendations with the VP, Tracy had prepared a 20-page document outlining all of her findings. Jada listened intently as Tracy shared all the details of her report and her final recommendation to invest. At the end of the presentation, when Tracy paused for breath, Jada asked, "What does the production manager think of your recommendation?" Tracy didn't have an answer. She hadn't spoken to the production manager. Jada recommended that she have a conversation and return to her.

Tracy was not looking forward to the conversation with Sam, the production manager. Her past meetings with him had not been productive. She met with him weekly to review the latest metrics, and his responses were rarely very detailed. He always seemed to always have crazy ideas that didn't feel practical and he would talk about the obstacles his team were facing. Her numbers didn't matter to him, no matter how much she tried to point out their importance.

The meeting with Sam to discuss the capital project went as predicted. When Tracy walked into his office, the first words out of his mouth were "I don't think we need to invest in a new machine. Our current yields are very good and it would take too much time to get the equipment installed and my team up to speed. It would take years to get the return we need." Tracy directed Sam to her charts, but he waved her off, dismissing her numbers as out-of-date and not relevant.

She left his office frustrated and went to speak to Jada about her concerns. "He won't listen to reason," she said. "I have shown him the yield improvements, but he doesn't believe me." Jada told her she didn't feel comfortable investing in the equipment without agreement from the production manager. Tracy left Jada's office uncertain about her next step.

Tracy is both a rational decision-maker and conflict assertive. Her typical style is the Fact Evangelist. These individuals typically make well thought-out decisions and are fact-based in their thinking but may miss information from others or struggle to get their thoughts across, especially when sharing with others who are not rational in their decision styles.

These individuals gather a lot of information, something which is important in decision-making, but they may be too convinced of the "correctness" of their facts to consider alternatives. When confronted, Tracy stuck to her data and did not address Sam's concerns. She also neglected to consider his perspective in her original proposal. Had she done so, she would have recognized the disconnect. She might have been able to find alternative data points or frame her messaging better to align to his concerns.

Benefits of this Style

- Your decisions are well thought-out.
- You demonstrate and role-model a thoughtful process of decision making.
- You bring new considerations and data points to decision making.

Risks of this Style

- You may take too much time to make decisions.
- Others may perceive you as a "know it all" who believes that your way is the best way.

- The team may not understand your thought process or get lost in too many facts.
- You may miss important information from others to inform your decisions.

Learning Some New Dance Moves

If your style is the Fact Evangelist, consider the following opportunities to balance your conflict style, extend your listening and move towards intuitive decision-making:

- Allow yourself to make decisions without all the information. Trust information from others.
- Shift your message away from the data and towards the desired shared outcome.
- Be sure to do listening checks with others when you are sharing ideas.

Dance Tips for Your Partners

If you are working with others who are Fact Evangelists, consider the following to effectively engage them in your decision process:

- Give them time to gather and disseminate data.
- When you have differing opinions, ask them to reflect back to you what they heard. This will ensure that they understand your perspective.
- Ask them to clarify their facts and help you understand the rationale behind their recommendations.

Leading a Tribe of Fact Evangelists

If your team is made up primarily of these individuals, you will want to think about the implications for decision-making.

Collectively this tribe can be dismissive of one another's ideas and can be competitive in trying to prove their own idea is right rather than considering other alternatives. They may also get lost in fact-finding missions, which will delay moving forward. To help this tribe:

- Allow this group to be thorough in their decision process but also be clear about deadlines. You will benefit from the quality and depth of their output.
- Ask them to reflect back what they heard from others in the team. Have them provide both sides of any argument, not just facts to support their own perspective.
- Align up front on the stakeholder inputs required to validate their recommendations.

An Army of Fact Evangelists

Cultures that embody this style are typically those based in science or which have a complex solution that is difficult to convey. They have strongly supported brand messaging, but they may slip in the market because they cannot react to new perspectives. They can get stuck in their own perceptions and miss changing market needs.

Research in Motion is a company that fell into this trap. In 1984, two young Canadian engineering graduates founded the company. They focused their research on developing two-way communication technologies, starting initially with workplace signs and pagers. They launched the BlackBerry in 1998. Co-CEO Jim Balsillie was the powerhouse behind promoting the brand, creating buzz within the technology community alongside the marketing agency, Lexicon Branding. In 2007, just prior to the launch of the first iPhone from Apple, Blackberry had nine million subscribers.

When the iPhone first launched, they dismissed it as a threat. Executives at RIM did not believe that the user experience would be positive without a keyboard. Even Microsoft's chief executive, Steve Ballmer, declared "there's no chance that the iPhone is going to get any significant market share."

RIM continued to push forward with marketing support, in particular for the new high-end BlackBerry Bold, which wasn't a touch-screen. Instead of re-evaluating the facts that made them successful in the past, they pushed forward with messaging that was no longer relevant.

The final blow came when they launched the Playbook, in response to the already successful iPad. Product availability lagged the marketing launch by six months. RIM lost momentum. When the

Playbook did hit the market, consumers were disappointed by the lack of functionality they had come to expect. RIM's efforts to react to changing market conditions came too late and in 2013, the Black-Berry smartphone ceased production.

Cultures dominated by Fact Evangelists have the opportunity to adapt and grow. Their decisions are rational but often focused inward instead of outward. To be successful, they need to be purposeful about questioning their own beliefs, which are biased by past success. They need to take risks that may not be fully supported by facts but that will allow them to move forward.

20. The Idea Holder

Tom is an HR manager who has led a team of HR generalists for the last two years. His company just completed its annual employee survey. Engagement numbers declined substantially, particularly in some teams. Tom's manager, Aryan, asked him to provide some suggestions on how to help managers improve engagement in their teams.

Tom immediately brought his team together to brainstorm some ideas. They came up with three new ways to engage employees: create an online forum for discussion; set up a competition that encourages employees to provide their ideas on innovation; and hold a mid-year celebration in addition to the annual year-end celebration. Tom knew the last idea would likely be costly, but the team was so enthusiastic about it, he thought it was worth suggesting to his manager.

Shortly after the team meeting, Tom heads excitedly into Aryan's office to show him the ideas that came out of it. Aryan asked Tom about why he chose those specific ideas. Tom explained that the team voted on the top ideas and these topped the vote. He believed that his team, as a representative of the employee population, likely reflected the needs of the organization in its excitement. Aryan questioned why Tom had focused on all employees and not those at the manager level, where scores were lowest in the survey. Tom hadn't considered that issue. Aryan suggested that Tom take a deeper look at results to highlight the areas that may require better focus.

Tom left the meeting deflated and concerned about how he would share the news with his team. The prospect of starting from scratch and digging further into the data did not excite him. He was certain that the ideas they came up with would resonate with the employees and help engagement. He was also not sure what it would take to convince his manager about the best course of action.

Tom is both an intuitive decision-maker and conflict averse. His typical style is the Idea Holder. These individuals typically make quick, instinct-based decisions. They tend to be good at listening to the inputs of others, but may struggle to challenge those ideas so as to maintain harmony in the team. These individuals also may miss important information as they rely more on experience than the data in front of them.

Idea Holders are usually good at collaboration, which is important to decision-making. They can also draw quickly on their experience to find relevant solutions. To be more successful, they should try to start the process with data to provide focus and rationales for the team. This would also allow them to reject or re-direct suggestions that don't align while not feeling confrontational.

Benefits of this Style
- You are able to make decisions quickly.
- You enhance team harmony in decision making.
- You help others to be innovative and think beyond the data.

Risks of this Style
- You may be missing important information to inform your decisions.
- Your ideas may be ignored because others don't understand the rationale behind them.
- You may disagree with decisions but keep quiet.

Learning Some New Dance Moves
If your style is that of the Idea Holder, consider the following opportunities to move into conflict and towards rational decision-making:

- Actively seek out information that counteracts your opinion.
- Share the rationale and thought process behind your message early on. Use facts when possible.
- Find opportunities to express yourself, even if in writing or one-on-one conversations.

Dance Tips for Your Partners

If you are working with others who are Idea Holders, consider the following steps to effectively engage them in your decision process:

- Consider their ideas, even if you don't understand the reasoning behind them. Encourage them to begin by stating the rationale.
- Ask them to provide a contradictory opinion. They may not willingly share it but could have a creative solution.
- Enable them to use different forms to communicate. They may not feel comfortable sharing in a group setting.

Leading a Tribe of Idea Holders

If your team is made up primarily of such individuals, you will want to think about the implications for decision making. They are likely to be harmonious and quick decision-makers but their ideas may not be backed up by facts. Among themselves, they may struggle to challenge one another and may also struggle to share and defend their ideas outside the team. To help this tribe:

- Allow this group to be creative in their decision process but also challenge the rationale behind it.
- Encourage this group to share ideas openly and seek data to support their hypotheses.
- Align up front on the data points required to validate their recommendations.

An Army of Idea Holders

Cultures that embody this style are typically innovative and supportive but may also struggle against change and in bringing new ideas to life. They may be quick to get new products or ideas to market, but effectiveness may be less than expected because of the lack of research prior to launch.

I recently worked with a client with a powerful brand and long-standing history. It was a known leader in many of the home care categories in which it played. The company asked me to help build out a customer story that would reflect a new future for the brand.

The goal of the story the client wanted to craft was to prove that it was a thought leader in its category and could bring new ideas to market. But it became quickly apparent to me that the company employees I was working with had lots of ideas about what the brand stood for and what to tell the customer, but very few facts to back up their beliefs.

We established a process that would allow for group discussion followed by individual work and then closing with more discussion to align on the final messages. Within this process, the group struggled to seek facts to support their ideas. I knew the company had invested in the data. They had the reports and the resources, but preferred instead to use visuals and statements to convey their message. As a result, the initial story felt simplistic and did not provide the kind of proof required to support the strength of the brand.

Cultures of this kind have an opportunity to move faster and with greater validation. Sometimes the requirement is to invest in data or research, but more often the opportunity is to strengthen the willingness to seek facts—and the skill to use those facts effectively—in order to support the desired message and build confidence in sharing it. Such teams need to see both challenging one another and using facts as an opportunity to strengthen their decisions. This process needs to be role-modelled and recognized by leaders.

21. The Passion Proclaimer

Kai is a marketing manager at an upscale boutique agency. The company recently landed a big contract with a company looking to advertise a new plant-based meat sauce. They appointed Kai the project lead. The team's first responsibility was to put together some initial concepts to present to the client. Kai was excited to be on the project team. Although he had never led a project before, he had been developing these types of campaigns over the past three years and felt confident that he could bring his A-game to the task.

Kai set up a kick-off meeting and shared with the team his expectations for the project. He talked about the project's importance and the fact that the team assembled were the best in the business. He could tell they were also excited to be working with a high-profile client. Kai suggested they meet again in a week when each designer, himself included, would pitch their concept.

When the next meeting came, Kai had assembled a powerful design. He kicked off the meeting with his concept and asked his fellow designers to showcase theirs. He realized that their concepts were more focused on the taste component of the messaging. His idea had highlighted the plant-based benefit. He knew from experience that this was a niche market and it would be important for the client to highlight this. He shared this thought with the team members and asked them to think about updating their designs to reflect this.

Once everyone had re-submitted their concepts, Kai brought them to Ingrid, the director of marketing, to prepare for the upcoming client meeting. Ingrid immediately expressed concern about the fact the element of taste was missing from the concepts. She told Kai that the designs were very creative, but the client brief was quite specific about taste being a prominent part of the message. She asked Kai to quickly re-think the concepts in time for the meeting.

Kai was disappointed that his concept did not resonate with his manager. He knew he should have taken a deeper look at the brief, but at the same time felt certain that his design concept would resonate more with consumers. He also felt the sting of failure at his first time as team lead. Clearly he had dismissed the other ideas too quickly. Now he had to re-read the brief, talk to the team members and quickly correct for his mistake.

Kai is both an intuitive decision maker and conflict assertive. His typical style is the Passion Proclaimer. These individuals typically make quick decisions based upon their initial instincts. They tend to be good at sharing ideas and getting others to follow, but may miss important information from others or from key data sources by moving too quickly or not allowing space for input. They also tend to turn quickly to past experience to find relevant solutions and often miss facts specific to the situation at hand. To be more successful, they should ask more questions to ensure they have thoroughly considered alternatives.

Benefits of this Style
- You are able to make decisions quickly.
- Team members see you as visionary.
- You bring new ideas and innovation to decision-making.

Risks of this Style
- You may be missing important information to inform your decision.
- Others may feel shut down or disregarded when you share your ideas.
- Your ideas may be ignored because others don't understand the rationale behind them.

Learning Some New Dance Moves
If your style is the Passion Proclaimer, consider the following opportunities to balance conflict with better listening and move towards rational decision-making:

- Actively seek out information that contradicts your opinion or ask others to share before you do.
- Be sure to do listening checks with others when you are sharing ideas.
- Share the rationale and thought process behind your message. Use facts when possible.

Dance Tips for Your Partners

If you are working with others who are Passion Proclaimers, consider the following ideas to effectively engage them in your decision process:

- Consider their ideas even if you don't understand the reasoning behind them.
- When you have a different opinion, ask them to reflect back to you what they heard. This will ensure that they understand your perspective.
- Respect their experience and the wisdom that comes from it but also be willing to challenge their assumptions.

Leading a Tribe of Passion Proclaimers

If your team is made up primarily of such individuals, you will want to think about the implications for decision-making. They are likely to move quickly on their collective ideas but may lack genuine evidence to support their plan. They may draw others along with their vision but not pause to ask for countervailing or contradictory data. Among themselves, they may compete over the best ideas and, lacking a clear rationale, the loudest voice may win. To help this tribe:

- Allow this group to be creative in their decision process but also challenge the rationale behind it. Consider inviting a guest who leans toward the rational decision-making approach to help them see what they can't see.
- As they communicate, ask each to reflect back what they heard from others in the team. Have them provide both sides of any argument, not just facts to support their own perspective.

- Align up front on the stakeholder inputs and data points required to validate their recommendations.

An Army of Passion Proclaimers

As a Canadian, I am familiar with the practice of cross-border shopping and so was familiar with Target which, until early 2013, only had stores in the U.S. Even before their Canadian launch, Target was a well-known brand in Canada. Canadians saw it as a premium place to shop, often pronouncing the chain's name as if it were a French word ("tar-JAY"). Canadians crossed the border to enjoy the treasure-hunt experience at Target and with expectations of better pricing than they found at home.

When Target launched in Canada, they went big, buying out Zellers, an existing national retailer with more than 270 locations. Half of these were transferred to other retailers or closed, leaving Target to renovate about 135 stores and re-open them under its own banner. The Zellers brand in Canada was not a strong one. The chain had been founded in 1931 and acquired by the Hudson's Bay Company in 1978. It peaked with more than 350 stores in 1999, but in subsequent years lost ground to Walmart's relentless Canadian expansion. Canadian shoppers viewed Zellers as a liquidation outlet with good prices but a poor shopping experience. Though Target attempted to renovate and restructure the former Zellers stores, more often than not it failed in its attempt. The store footprint was often smaller than the average Target store in the U.S. The "new" stores might carry the Target brand but to Canadians they still looked like Zellers. Worse yet, the stores lacked inventory and prices were higher than expected. The brand did not at all resemble the experience Canadians had experienced on their cross-border shopping forays.

Less than two years after launch, Target announced its retreat from Canada. The failed expansion cost the company $1.2 billion. Experts attribute the failure of Target Canada to poor planning and overambitious expectations. Retailers know that customer connection within the first three months of launch is essential, but Target did not plan to make this happen. Rather than initially launch in a small number of stores and focus on replicating their brand with Canadian consumers, they jumped in the deep end on a misguided conviction that Canadians would flock to Target stores on the strength of brand name alone.

Target relied on its past experience and plowed boldly ahead. They did not devote enough time or careful thought to how the brand experience could be successfully replicated in Canada. They had the opportunity to take smaller steps, to launch in a few stores and pause to consider the reaction by Canadian consumers. Instead they were blinded by their past success.

Cultures dominated by Passion Proclaimers need to take the opportunity to slow down and consider alternatives. Reliance on past experience is not enough. They need to balance confidence with caution. Many companies which have had initial success with game-changing innovation struggle to replicate that success. Those who have experienced past success must consider how a new situation might be different.

22. Moving Within Truth

When I was in my late twenties, I did my first MBTI assessment. This Myers-Briggs methodology identifies what personality type you are born with; it defines your preferences. One area that is measured is your tendency to be either "Thinking" or "Feeling" in how you make decisions. The spectrum is similar to my measure of rational vs. intuitive decision-making. The primary difference is the consideration of emotion. People who fall towards "Thinking" tend to be logical and impersonal when weighing a decision. Those who fall towards the "Feeling" side are more likely to consider people and emotions when arriving at a conclusion.

I landed quite far toward the "Thinking" end of the spectrum. The result resonated with me and was further confirmed when I was asked to do a task with other "Thinkers." We were supposed to be coaches on a competitive team who had to determine which players would play in the final game. Only 15 of the 20 players on the team would play. We needed a plan on how we would decide who would take part and who would not. As logical, "Thinking" people, we devised a ranking strategy based on a set of criteria. This would determine who got their place on the team. One man got up to transcribe our criteria on the flip-chart. It was clear that he was not able to keep up with the barrage of ideas we threw at him. The group suggested that he sit down and give the marker to another woman who might "get what we were saying" faster. He did so. She got up and we finished the task. We had a nicely ranked list of players who would make up our top 15 based on a clearly defined list of success criteria.

After the exercise was complete, the facilitator did two things; she asked how we felt about the exercise, and she compared the results and approach to the other group (made up of "Feelers"). The first realization was that as we did the exercise, we were not thinking about how it felt. We were trying to accomplish the task. Upon reflection, I realized the harshness of the way we had operated. I mentioned that we told our first moderator to sit down when he didn't get it. We did not consider his feelings, only the logical way in which we needed to accomplish the task. Thankfully, he took minimal offence but agreed that hadn't been the best feeling. Had he been conflict averse, we would have totally shut him down.

The second revelation was in how the other team approached the task. Instead of creating a ranking based on success criteria as we did, their idea was to ask the team about how to decide. They engaged them and collaborated to find a "fair" solution. They didn't have a well-organized list, but instead a brilliant idea on how to get everyone aligned to a common solution. Their result was likely to involve less heartache than ours. They considered the truth of others.

This was one of my first lessons on how to do things differently. It had not even occurred to me to do the task a different way. I was working with my logical brain. Nor had it occurred to me that we were harsh in how we handled the discussion until I was asked to reflect upon it. This was a good lesson in the power of pausing.

In 2019, I redid my MBTI. The result shocked me. I shifted so substantially down the spectrum that I was now classified as "Feeling." At first, I believed the test result was wrong and found another online version to complete. Same result. When I looked at the spectrum, I landed only slightly over the Feeling line, but it was still a monumental shift from where I had been in my twenties. Somehow throughout my career I had developed feelings!

What caused this shift? The developers of the Myers-Briggs tests will tell you that your preferences should remain unchanged, but I believe we are shaped by experience. With age, I believe I understood the importance of other perspectives more than ever before. In my work, my facilitation skills and listening skills became more important than my expertise. My recognition of the benefits of involving others deepened. And I had just gone through two life-changing events—the loss of my dad and the near-death of my husband. More than ever, the logical, rational way of thinking was not my only problem-solving tool. I had new tools in my toolbox. I could no longer rely on myself to solve world problems.

I now recognize that *my* truth is not *the* truth. I still land far from the middle in this assessment. I am a Fact Evangelist and therefore too assertive and overly rational at times. I know that I still have lots of opportunity to silence the logical arguments playing out in my head and to keep quiet instead of always speaking up. Recognizing my bias is still difficult, as is opening my mind to diverse perspectives, but my goal is to get a little better each day.

Assessments are intended to put us into buckets, but they do not define who we are or who we can become. They help us question our way of thinking to improve how we work with others. For me assessments are a wonderful spotlight on why I behave the way I do and a reminder that the way I think and process information may be different from others. But we don't live in buckets. Our actions are often dictated by our circumstances. Our experiences shape which way we lean. If you naturally lean towards one area of the spectrum in conflict or decision-making or thinking and feeling, you can move the other way. You can pause and think about which way you *should* move, which way you *want* to move. Every one of us has the opportunity to choose and change how we behave.

Truth Warriors recognize that success depends on their ability to move towards the middle, balancing rational and intuitive styles and leaning in and out of conflict. In writing this book, I spoke to several leaders about what makes them successful. Although each fell into different quadrants in this model, they had one common theme. Each indicated that a shift across the spectrum was key to their success. Those who claimed they had been rational decision-makers found themselves being more intuitive. Those who were originally more assertive found themselves resisting the urge to express their own opinions and being more inclusive of others. The reverse was also true. The strength of their leadership and decision-making ability was not a reflection of where they landed on this model, but instead of how they moved within it. The dance they learned helped them to know when to be the Scout and when to be the Soldier. They learned how to balance the paradox of truth-seeking and truth-speaking. They learned to lead truth.

PART FIVE

Lead Truth: Building Your Battle Cry

23. The Battle Before You

This battle you are facing as you navigate complex decisions is one that many leaders have fought before. The battle does not end. It is an ongoing fight against ourselves to do better, be better. It is the fight against our natural bias and our reactions when others disagree with us. It is the recognition that the truth we seek and the truth we speak is not ours alone.

We must be purposeful on how to fight this battle. We must arm ourselves with the right weapons, but wield them carefully. We must embrace the dance, recognizing the need to move alongside others and outside of ourselves.

Truth Warriors recognize the paradox required to lead. They must be willing to let go of their understanding and of their judgements and also to build up, creating structures and rewards to enable their teams. They must create harmony through trust and commonality, and create tension with diversity and transparent dialogue. They must be humble but with courage as well as bold by taking risks and recognizing bravery in others.

24. Let Go and Build Up

"Science is always wrong. It never solves a problem without creating ten more." — Albert Einstein

In his TED talk, "The Pursuit of Ignorance," Stuart Firestein explains the importance of ignorance in the quest for knowledge and as a key part of scientific discovery. His description of ignorance is not intended to be negative. Instead he describes it as "a communal gap in our knowledge, something that's just not there to be known or isn't known well enough yet or we can't make predictions from."

He explains that the art of science and the role of scientists centres not on how much you know, but instead on the awareness of how much you have yet to learn. The stereotypical model of scientific discovery, he explains, assumes that scientists have all the facts and therefore can find a solution. Instead, he compares science to a magic well, where every time we fill our bucket with water, it fills up again.

The lesson in this for leaders is to recognize that you will never have all the facts. If you think you do, you are wrong. Your role as a leader should be to help understand the questions left to be answered. The most difficult decisions will never be 100 percent certain. By acknowledging our inability to know everything, we are able to move forward.

Truth Warriors recognize their own blind spots and acknowledge their bias. They know that the only certainty is uncertainty and that there will always be more to learn and more data to be found. In decision-making, if you don't recognize this reality, you will either move forward with unfounded confidence or be paralyzed by feeling that you don't know enough. Neither of these positions will generate good decisions. Instead, Truth Warriors know when to say we have enough information to move forward. They know how to play in the grey.

"I am not here to be right. I am here to get it right."
—Brené Brown

Play in the grey.

Annie Duke is a poker champion and self-proclaimed "uncertainty evangelist." Her book *Thinking in Bets* is a guide on how to be comfortable with uncertainty and a reminder about the importance of probabilities when we make decisions. She offers an example of a poker game where she was acting as a colour commentator. It was an all-in moment. Two players laid all their cards on the table and betting had stopped. It was Annie's role to share the probability of each player winning given the current set of cards on the table. Annie predicted that one player had a 76 percent chance of winning and the other had a 24 percent chance. The last cards were dealt and as it turns out, the player with the 24 percent likelihood of winning was the one who won the hand. Someone in the crowd proclaimed, "Annie, you were wrong!" and she explained why she wasn't. "I said that outcome would happen 24 percent of the time. That's not zero. You got to see part of the 24 percent."

Decisions are like poker. We cannot possibly predict the future. We can only hope to have a positive result more often than a negative one. Sometimes the outcome results from chance or unforeseen circumstance. We need to stop thinking of decisions as absolutes of right and wrong. More importantly, we need to stop thinking of people as right or wrong, and instead consider their perspectives as being on a different position on the spectrum. As Annie implies, if we express our opinions as a level of confidence, any change in this measurement would not be an acknowledgment of defeat but instead a shift in thinking. If I currently feel 60 percent confident in my understanding, and I change this to 40 percent, I do not have to say I was wrong. I can allow others the same opportunity. This approach would enable someone to change their opinion without feeling prosecuted. It removes the emotionally charged feeling that comes with letting go of your belief and acknowledging those of others. It removes personal judgement. If we can be open to shifting along the spectrum of our opinion as opposed to the hard stop of "right vs. wrong," we can make the discussion of alternatives less personal.

Truth Warriors avoid the absolutes of right and wrong. Instead, they recognize that decision-making and beliefs should be considered on a spectrum. They consider probabilities and risks within their decisions and recognize that sometimes chance plays an unfortunate role. They let go of judgement and know that sometimes to speed up they need to slow down.

Rush slower.

"I don't have the time to rush anymore."
—Unknown

My mother had double-bypass heart surgery when she was 45 years old. Like my father, she had smoked for most of her life. Unlike him, she made a plan to quit. The bypass surgery itself was not enough to inspire her, but it certainly was a nudge in the right direction. Ten years later she smoked her last cigarette. Her strategy was to approach quitting with baby steps. The idea of never having another cigarette was too daunting. Instead, she made her plan for the day. She would say, "I will not have a cigarette today." The next day she would say the same thing. Each day was a choice and never did she state, "I will *never* have a cigarette again." She focused her willpower on small wins. Each day was an achievement. There were days later in the process when she almost caved, but she was able to push herself to get through the day. The days turned into weeks, at which point she was past the physical addiction. Mentally the desire was still there. She reminded herself that if she were to smoke now, it would actually be an unpleasant experience. Weeks turned into months and months turned into years. She is now able to be around friends who smoke with minimal desire to do so.

My mother was successful because she took baby steps towards a bigger goal. In decision-making, we need to be courageous and systematic. Both are easier to do in smaller steps.

Microbravery is the process of taking "small, everyday risks that take us out of our personal comfort zones." It allows us to take small steps towards bigger goals. This is a common way to combat anxiety. My son was having difficulty falling asleep by himself. Rather than go cold turkey, we devised a plan to reward his microbravery. The first night we would sit just outside his door where he could see us. The next night we would sit outside his door, but out of sight. He could call to us if necessary. The night after that we sat completely out of earshot but still on the same floor. Eventually he was able to sleep entirely on his own. Moving slowly and with smaller steps allowed us to accomplish the goal faster.

In their book *Decisive*, Chip and Dan Heath talk about slowing down decision-making in a similar way. They call this an "ooch," which is a term they learned from working with a company called National Instruments. It is a combination of the words "inch" and "scoot" and its purpose is to allow one to conduct small experiments to test hypotheses. The Heaths describe it as "firing bullets and then cannonballs." It is a process to test the water, create hypotheses and refine. It's agile decision-making.

It might be tempting to think that considering more alternatives would slow down decision-making. In fact, research suggests that this is not the case. Kathleen Eisenhardt studied top leadership teams in Silicon Valley. Her evidence suggests that fast decision-makers use more, not less, information, than do slow decision-makers. They also examine more, not fewer, alternatives. She also found that conflict resolution is critical to decision speed.

One factor that seemed to contribute to this success was access to real-time information rather than simple planning information during the decision-making process. Executives engaged more directly with lower-level employees in roundtable forums. This allowed them to identify issues quickly. It also offered them the opportunity to develop an intuitive understanding of the situation, recognizing patterns through continued exposure.

Faster moving companies also considered alternatives simultaneously. One of these companies described the following method of considering options:

1. Propose a sincere alternative.
2. Support someone else's alternative, even when actually opposing it.
3. Propose an insincere alternative, one that the proposer does not actually support.

Conversely, slower moving companies often considered only one option and searched for a new one only when the first was no longer considered feasible. This slowed down the decision-making process and made them more likely to make the wrong decision when the pressure was on.

Analysis paralysis is another risk in decision-making. This is particularly true for those who are rational decision-makers. We get stuck when we feel we need more information before moving forward. It is tempting to allow timelines to dictate your decision making. Deadlines can force you to gather information until you run out of time. But what if you don't have a set timeline? Decision-makers need to set themselves artificial deadlines to avoid this. What would be a stretch and what would be more realistic? Aim for the stretch. It is easy to procrastinate when feeling overwhelmed by a decision. Forcing yourself to act and having others hold you accountable to deadlines will be important to avoid inaction.

Truth Warriors know they need to slow down to speed up. They take baby steps and ooch before they leap. Bravery is a muscle they strengthen over time. They consider alternatives simultaneously and in real time. They build intuition through rational data-gathering and set optimistic timelines to achieve their goals. They know how to engage others in the process and help their audience to understand information. They help to simplify the complex.

Simplify the complex.

"If you dismiss the individual concerns, the science won't matter." —*Barack Obama*

In his TEDx Talk "Quantum Physics for 7-Year-Olds" Dominic Walliman explains how to simplify complex concepts. It starts by understanding the audience. When teaching quantum physics to children, Walliman knows that their knowledge will be limited. He starts by providing context to bring them all to the same level of understanding and constantly checks in to confirm they are understanding each step in the discussion. If you are trying to share your message with others, then you need to start with where they are. Understand their level and set expectations at the start.

Secondly, Walliman cautions us to avoid too much depth when explaining a challenging concept. It is a common mistake to want to explain facts in detail. Just because you put the work in to find out all those details does not mean you need to showcase them. Be clear on your message and the main takeaways. Customize your content to those relevant details and leave others in the appendix or your back pocket.

Walliman also recognizes that importance of clarity over accuracy. Obviously, Walliman will not be able to share all the intricate details of physics to children, but he still gets across his message. He suggests using simpler words and examples of concepts that may not be completely accurate but are more understandable. For example, he uses the word "spin" to explain what an MRI machine does with your atoms. In reality, it does not actually work that way, but it painted a visual picture that helped me (and the children) to understand the concept. Be clear that your language is simple and descriptive and talks to the audience at their level of understanding.

Lastly, simplifying the complex is about passion and enthusiasm. Talk about why this is relevant to you personally or why it's important or interesting. Don't make me figure it out for myself with facts and figures. Think about the headline. What is the hook that will catch my attention? We listen to messages we find interesting.

Truth Warriors know how to take complex data and make it relevant and digestible. It stems from their passion and is obvious in their enthusiasm. Ego can get in the way of simplifying the complex. It doesn't matter if the message is completely accurate or that all the facts are there to prove your point. The goal is to connect with your audience, be relevant, and help them understand. It starts with solving the right problem.

Solve the right problem.

"We don't need to fight every alligator. We need to cross the swamp." —*Geeta Sankappanavar*

I had a client who wanted to move into new markets. They were selling food and the countries they were considering had strict and inconsistent regulatory guidelines. They began the exercise by identifying all the countries they could move into, based on population size and how under-developed their sector was in that country. Thailand was one country that rose to the top of this list. When they dug a little deeper into the possibility of shipping goods to Thailand, they realized that country had banned one of the ingredients they used in their manufacturing process. They decided to take Thailand off their list.

When I asked them about the rationale for the decision, they explained the situation. I asked them some more questions to better understand their thinking. Was it a substantial opportunity? Yes. Could they run the process without the chemical? They hadn't thought about that. When considering obstacles, they thought in black and white. "The chemical is banned and we use the chemical, therefore it is not an option." I challenged them to think about the problem differently.

It is easy when we are problem solving to get stuck in our traditional models. Too often we jump to "obvious" solutions before we truly understand the problem we are trying to solve. We take mental shortcuts and answer an easier question when we should be considering a bigger, more complex question. For my client, getting into the Thai market was a "go"/"no-go" decision with only one criterion. Instead, they needed to branch out their thinking to ask questions like "Why is it banned?" "Are there substitutes that would be equally effective?" "Why are we using the chemical? "Can we change our process?" Once they asked these important questions, the problem changed from "How do we find countries to ship in our existing product" to "How do we meet the needs of countries that need our product." This allowed them to see all the options.

Defining the problem is a key step in any decision. The "5 Whys" is a simple approach that I have used to do this. You start with the problem and continue to ask "why?" until you understand the root cause. This is often the first step in trying to make the right decision.

 I saw this best (and simply) explained in a video by Jerilyn Edginton called "The Jefferson Memorial and the 5 Whys." She modernized the original content by the Juran Institute. The problem started when a crumbling piece of cement fell off the Jefferson Memorial, almost injuring a tourist. The first "why" was: "Why is it crumbling?" It was determined that the soap used on the monument was reacting with jet exhaust from the nearby airport. Had they had stopped with that first "why," then the solution might have been to remove the airport. Clearly this would not have been feasible.

The next "why" was: "Why is the Memorial being washed so frequently with such strong soap?" The answer to that question was "the pigeons." The Memorial seemed to attract a large number of pigeons. Why was that? They came for the spiders. Why the spiders? They came for the midges. Midges are tiny insects that are attracted to water. They come out of ground around dusk to breed and then die, becoming spider food. So why the midges? They were attracted to the floodlights around the Monument that were switched on around dusk. The solution: Delay turning on the lights until after sunset, a step that reduced the midge population by 90 percent. This, in turn, reduced the number of the spiders and therefore the number of pigeons and therefore the need to clean the monument as rigorously. The end result? A simple solution to what could have been a very expensive problem.

Truth Warriors start with the problem. They consider alternatives by asking "why" and delve into the root cause before making a decision. They think more broadly and ask questions about the true nature of the problem they are trying to solve. They recognize the importance of a systematic process for decision-making. They reward the path for making decisions, and not the outcome.

<table>
<tr><td>

Reward the path.

</td><td>

"Success is a journey, not a destination. The doing is often more important than the outcome."
— *Arthur Ashe*

</td></tr>
</table>

In preparing for the 2016 Olympics, Michael Phelps participated in an interview with NBC's Bob Costas, who asked Phelps how it would feel to finish with a silver medal instead of a gold. "Would that haunt you?" Although clearly Phelps desired to win gold, his answer was, "No, because I know I could look back at how I prepared and I would know that we did whatever we could do to prepare to be the best." Michael Phelps acknowledges the importance of rewarding the process instead of the outcome.

In decision-making, we often make the mistake of evaluating the results of the decision based on the outcome and thereby do not acknowledge or learn from the steps we took to get there. We can have done everything possible to understand a decision before making it, and its results can be unexpected. Conversely, we can make decisions on the fly and get lucky with the result.

Most businesses did not plan for the pandemic of 2020. It would not have been built into a contingency plan or even considered a risk. There is no way the world could have known that its workforce would now be mostly remote, the supply chain would be disrupted or that consumer behaviours and perceptions would change. I saw a virtual presentation from the CEO of WestJet. Revenues had dropped 95 percent. Nothing could have prepared them for that. I also did some work for a disinfecting company. Their sales had nearly doubled. Some companies won and others lost.

In January 2020, a client I worked with had been experiencing substantial growth and believed that the size of his current team would not allow him to support his desired future state. Given that his lease was up in February, he wondered if now was the time to make more room for his growing team. He sought alternative space. He ran models to examine the return, considering the renovations that would also need to take place. He spoke to others in his field to understand the risks. He mapped out the best- and worst-case revenue scenarios to ensure that he could cover the cost of the new investment. He even negotiated a cash-back option that would cover the cost of the renovation as part of the lease terms. Everything looked sound. He signed a lease in February 2020. A ten-year lease.

In March 2020, the world went in to lockdown and his entire team began to work from home. By the end of the summer, they had yet to return and now realized the benefits of this new arrangement. More space was no longer needed. Would you call his investment a bad decision? Ultimately, the result was unfortunate, but the process to get there was solid. Should he have made a different choice? If your answer is yes, then you are judging him on the outcome and not the process by which he made the decision.

Process accountability involves rewarding the effort to achieve outcomes. Outcome accountability rewards the effectiveness of delivering the outcome. Academic research has shown that increasing process accountability leads to superior judgment quality in a variety of tasks and that outcome accountability can have negative effects on performance. When held accountable after a decision is made, employees are more likely to rationalize and justify their decisions. They will be more likely to defend their beliefs and develop stronger opinions about why they were right. The result is that we are less likely to course-correct when required. Conversely, if we reward the decision process rather than the outcome, we will be open to trying a new path.

The first step in rewarding the process is to put mechanisms in place to evaluate a decision before it takes place. One leader I spoke to shared his approach. When making team decisions, he invites someone chosen at random from outside the decision-making team to offer their perspective. Their opinion is fresh and less likely to be biased. It is also a great way of checking to make sure that groupthink hasn't taken the team in the wrong direction.

Leaders must also recognize the type of contributions being made. Is the information being presented accurate and well thought-out? Do the team members have facts to back up their recommendations? It will be key to test for assumptions as opposed to facts. Some people are great at positioning opinions as truth.

I teach a course on providing feedback. In it, I show the class a video of a manager berating an employee. I ask the class afterwards to tell me what they observed. I typically get answers like "He was rude to his employee," "He was a bad manager," and "The employee was disengaged." This is when I challenge them to think about the difference between judgement and observation. Observations would be "The manager raised his voice," "The dialogue took place in a public place," and "The employee leaned away from the manager." These observations are undisputable. Just as when providing feedback, when evaluating decisions it is essential to understand where a statement is based on opinion or fact.

To test for fact vs. opinion, consider questions like:

- What is the source of that information?
- How do you know that to be true?
- Do you have an example of how this worked before?

Leaders must also consider the type of contributions made as part of the pre-decision process. Were the team members objective and open-minded? Were diverse perspectives considered? Are the right people in the room? Have we considered all the alternatives?

A good way to evaluate a decision is to assume that the outcome is poor. A pre-mortem is one way to achieve this. In a post-mortem, the goal is to understand what went wrong after disaster has occurred. In the case of a pre-mortem, you attempt to understand what went wrong before the scenario actually plays out, or, in the case of decision-making, what *could* go wrong. Carrying out a pre-mortem causes us to envision a different future—one in which the decision we are about to make has a poor outcome. A study by Mitchell, Russo, and Pennington in 1989 demonstrated that judgement improved and you were 30 percent more likely to identify the reasons for a future outcome if you imagined that an event had already occurred.

As part of this process we look into the future, assume the project has failed, and ask:

- What caused this to happen?
- What might have been a better path?
- What information were we missing?
- If we had made a different decision, what might have happened?
- What should we have done differently?

There will still be an opportunity to evaluate a decision after it is made, ideally to course-correct or to learn from it. When evaluating a situation *after* a decision is made, consider both the outcome and the process to get there. This matrix might help.

The ideal end state is at the top right. We achieved what we set out to do and our thinking about what was needed to get there was sound. In the top left corner, the process was good but the outcome was bad. When this happens, there is an opportunity to understand why. Were there factors that we didn't consider? Did some risks that we anticipated come to fruition? Were there unexpected internal or external market conditions? The most important questions are: *What can we learn from this? Is there something we can change in our decision-making process for the next time?*

The riskiest quadrant in this model is the bottom right: bad process and good outcome. This result leads us to believe that the way in which we made the decision was optimal. Instead of recognizing that we "got lucky" we believe that we deserved the positive and that we did all the proper planning.

The least favourable outcome is clearly the bottom left quadrant. This is the one which requires the most change. If we use this opportunity to evaluate the process by which we made the decision, it might allow us to put better structures in place for next time. Be careful not to justify the result as bad luck.

Truth Warriors control systems, not outcomes. They put mechanisms in place to avoid mistakes and focus on the accuracy of data within decision-making. They put procedures in place to prevent groupthink and avoid blind spots. They value diverse perspectives. They reward the path, not the destination. They hold their team accountable for the process, not the outcome. They role-model and recognize those who bring accuracy to the discussion and are open-minded and courageous in their decision-making process. They create harmony and tension.

25. Create Harmony and Tension

"The best way to find out if you trust somebody is to trust them." —*Ernest Hemingway*

My father was a likable, charismatic man. He started his life as a mechanic but spent most of his years in sales. As a child, I would ask him what he sold. His true business was selling warranty packages to car dealerships, but he would always answer my question with the statement, "I sell an idea." Although I hadn't intended it, my path followed his and I, too, ended up in sales. Although I had heard him say what he sold many times over the years, I didn't see myself as selling an "idea." I was selling telecom equipment or cosmetics or pet food and as a young salesperson, I believed I had to convince my buyers why they should buy my product instead of someone else's. I did so by showing them the facts. The facts about why my product was better or why they were missing out or how big the opportunity was.

As my experience in sales grew, I started to understand that I was not just selling telecom equipment or cosmetics or pet food. Facts were not enough. This became even more true when I started my own business. I was now selling myself. I was selling an idea. Building relationships and developing trust became the cornerstone of my success. It didn't matter how many testimonials or examples of the work there were. I had to sell myself. If they didn't trust me, then it wouldn't matter. My dad was one of my biggest advocates in starting my own business. He was also my greatest sales coach. He was not a fact-based seller. He had a high school diploma and mechanic's hands when he started in sales. He was successful because people trusted him. He knew how to build and nurture relationships. This was the skill I was missing. It came easily to him. He would actually chuckle at me when I asked him, "How do you get people to believe you?"

After he retired, he wanted to keep working. Retirement did not suit him, and he wanted to keep busy. He also didn't want to stray far from home. The appliance store across the street from his house was looking for a salesman. Although he grumbled about the pay cut, you could tell being back in the game re-invigorated him. He would share stories about how he told someone what *not* to buy. Instead, he would guide them to the best products for their purpose and if he didn't have the right product, he would encourage them to shop elsewhere. Oftentimes that resulted in a long-term customer. He built trust by behaving in a counterintuitive manner.

One of the best ways to get others to trust you is to trust them first. Extending trust creates reciprocity: when you trust people, others tend to trust you in return. Much of the time, reduced trust is a result of misunderstanding. The only way to break down that wall is through better understanding. Trust is the foundation for open dialogue and sets the stage to promote diverse thought and innovative ideas. That is the foundation for better decisions.

The Trust Equation, which is discussed in the book *The Trusted Advisor*, by Maister, Green and Galford, is a good tool to understand how leaders can demonstrate trust. It consists of three components that build trust: credibility, reliability and intimacy. It is expressed like this:

$$\text{Trust} = \frac{\text{Credibility} + \text{Reliability} + \text{Intimacy}}{\text{Self Orientation}}$$

Credibility is the easiest quality to demonstrate. It is based on your expertise. In decision-making, it relates to the facts and sources of your information. Reliability is demonstrated over time. Can you be counted on to deliver against your promises? This shows up in the process of decision-making. Are you holding people accountable as to how they show up? Are you consistent in how you allow for mistakes? Then there is intimacy. This takes longer to build and is about emotional closeness. Is your team willing to have difficult conversations and do they trust that the results will not be punitive? As a leader, building trust through intimacy requires you to be vulnerable and authentic. Finally, down there in the denominator, the last element of trust is self-orientation. This is a demonstration that you care more about others' agenda than your own. Leaders can provide evidence of this by asking more questions, listening to alternatives and working towards a common agenda.

Trust is essential for good team decision-making. One CEO described it well when she told me that "the only way I feel like people follow based on your decisions is if you have created a good foundation of trust." A big part of this for her was recognizing positive intention. Even in uncomfortable situations, or when relaying unfortunate information, if the intention is good, it will allow others to hear you better. In order to inspire change and bring people along the journey, you need them to trust you. To encourage everyone to contribute, to feel safe to express themselves, they must trust you.

Truth Warriors build a foundation of trust through their own behaviours. They know that the best way to gain trust is to demonstrate it first. It requires them to be vulnerable and authentic and to hold team members accountable for their actions. In decision making, they don't pit team members against either other. They don't promote an "Us vs. Them" mentality. Instead, they recognize the need for "Us *and* Them."

Recognize the need for Us *and* Them.

"We must learn to live together as brothers or we will perish together as fools."
—Dr. Martin Luther King, Jr.

In 2020, racial tension came to a boil with the killing of George Floyd. In response, some people started looting and rioting. Different "sides" of the argument raged on the internet. The mayor of Atlanta, Keisha Lance Bottoms, a Black woman, called on looters and rioters to "Stop burning down our community." She reminded the population that when they did so, they were impacting the lives of Black store owners and Black families.

Others took to the internet to defend the rioting. I saw a powerful video from another Black woman named Kimberly Jones. She explained the "why" behind the looting and rioting. She compared society to a game of Monopoly. If you played Monopoly against someone for 400 rounds, never won, had to hand over any money you made after every round you lost, it would be impossible to ever catch up and start winning. This was the result of slavery and Black oppression. They haven't caught up and the only way to catch up and have any shot at winning the game is through a different distribution of wealth and a system that allows for unequal opportunity in *their* favour. That is the only way to level the playing field. Jones's response to the mayor who said "Stop burning down our community" was "It's not *our* community."

These women are sitting on different sides of the riot argument. One of them is trying to explain the anger of the community. The other is trying to deter it. Both truths can be true. Both of these Black women ultimately believe in the same thing: equality for their people. Both want a safe community and a way forward from systemic racism. Imagine if these powerful women could work together towards that cause, rather than oppose one another.

Perceptions around law enforcement are causing another divide. Police are trying to defend themselves, while others are trying to showcase police corruption. Social media is flooded with every good and bad thing a police officer has done. Those who are posting pictures of cops doing good things are trying to prove that bad cops are in the minority. Those who post pictures of cops doing bad things are trying to prove that the system is broken. Although both truths seem counterintuitive, both can be true. There can be good cops in a broken system.

 Religion is another area where we hold tightly to our beliefs. It has been the cause of many conflicts. And yet, when we compare two seemingly different religions, we can find similarities. A Venn diagram is a great tool to represent both the differences and commonalities between two beliefs. The diagram below compares Christian and Muslim perspectives. It demonstrates that although these religions often feel substantially different, many practices and beliefs are common to both.

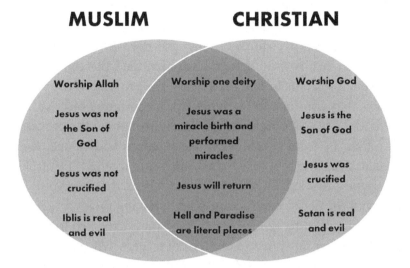

MUSLIM   CHRISTIAN

Worship Allah — Worship one deity — Worship God

Jesus was not the Son of God — Jesus was a miracle birth and performed miracles — Jesus is the Son of God

Jesus was not crucified — Jesus will return — Jesus was crucified

Iblis is real and evil — Hell and Paradise are literal places — Satan is real and evil

Our truths often lead us down an "Us vs. Them" path. We hold strong to our beliefs and rather than consider the war we are both trying to win, we fight our individual battles. We try to prove that we are right and they are wrong. If we can stop taking sides and instead look towards a common goal, we can make better decisions.

As part of her book, *The Good Fight*, Liane Davey shares a technique called "Two Truths" that works well for this purpose. The fundamental principle of this technique is that we can both be right. It starts with acknowledgement and understanding of the other person's perspective. You must avoid the temptation to contradict their belief. Each party declares their belief. The other party acknowledges it. You use questions to try to understand each other's overall objectives. You then look for a solution that supports both of you.

If both the mayor and Ms. Jones did this exercise, it might start with the statements "Rioting is destructive" and "Rioting is necessary to get attention." The next step would be to ask enough questions to understand what they are trying to solve. Ms. Jones might begin by saying, "We are trying to get the government to see that something must be done now." Mayor Bottoms would likely agree with that need. She might then tell Ms. Jones that she is concerned for the safety of the people in the community. Ms. Jones likely has a similar concern. What they might both realize through this conversation is that they do share the same goals. Their methods may differ but they are on the same side of the fight. It doesn't need to be Us vs. Them but instead Us *and* Them working together.

When making decisions, leaders also need to understand how aligned their teams are. If they have identified the right problem and have put systems in place to reward the process, the next step is to ensure they continue to work towards a common objective. They need to identify and validate alternatives throughout the process. To ensure that the team continues to feel engaged and valued, leaders must check in. One tool I have used to do this is called "Fist to Five." After a good discussion, the leader can check that everyone is on board with the decision or action-plan by asking each participant to indicate their "Fist to Five." Each participant is expected to raise one hand with either a fist or the number of fingers that represent their alignment to the decision. A fist (or zero) means completely not aligned. Five fingers means completely aligned. Typically, if someone holds up fewer than four fingers, you will need to understand why and continue the dialogue to get to a point where everyone has either four or five fingers raised.

Truth Warriors look for commonality in the problems they are trying to solve. They know that differing beliefs can coexist under a common goal. By finding the "why" behind the various truths and testing for ongoing alignment, they can bring people together. They avoid the temptation to hold too tight to their own perspective and instead respect differences of opinion and thought. They know when to try a new approach to achieve their goals.

"She stood in the storm, and when the wind did not blow her way, she adjusted her sails."
—*Elizabeth Edwards*

Try a new approach.

I have learned a lot from my kids. I have three and each is very different. Each also has a bit of me in them. My oldest son taught me a wonderful lesson once. I was taking my kids to the corner store for a Slushy. At that time, they were 4, 6 and

9 years old. Before we left on the one-kilometre trek, I asked how they wanted to travel, by bike or on foot. The older boys (6 and 9) wanted to ride their bikes. My daughter (then 4) decided to walk. I tried to encourage her to bike along with her brothers but she was insistent. (She gets her stubbornness from me.) We set off. About halfway in to the trip, the boys had ridden slightly ahead and stopped at the lights to wait for us to catch up. They couldn't hear me and I was nervous about them crossing the busy road without us. I had to wait for my daughter's tiny legs to cover the distance. All of a sudden, seeing how fast her brothers were getting there, she declared: "I want to bike." I told her that we didn't have her bike with us and that she needed to walk. "No, I need to bike," she insisted. Obviously, her request was illogical and I was getting frustrated by her insistence and my inability to do anything about it. I told her she needed to keep walking or we would go home. She sat down. She was not going anywhere without a bike. I had no bike to provide, and very little patience. I yelled at her to "get up" and told her that unless she did, she would not get a Slushy. And then something happened. In the middle of my temper tantrum, my older son showed up. He had biked back and had asked his younger brother to join him. He asked why we weren't moving and I told him, "Your sister wants to bike and I can't get her to move." He calmly said to her, "Do you want us to get off our bikes and walk with you?" She said "Yes" and they did. Everyone got Slushies.

Many businesses have had to adapt and try new approaches to be successful. YouTube was originally launched as an online dating site called "Tune In, Hook Up." It allowed people to upload videos of themselves talking about the person they wanted to date. The concept did not take off but the idea of having a venue for anybody to upload videos did. They quickly pivoted and launched YouTube in April 2005. By March 2006, it had 25 million videos uploaded and was generating around 20,000 uploads a day.

Truth Warriors know that there is always a different way and maybe even a better way. They actively seek out new approaches. They learn from their failures and consider re-direction. They engage others and are open-minded to a different course of action. They know the importance of considering diverse perspectives. They can build different ducks.

Build different ducks.

"It is not our differences that divide us. It is our inability to recognize, accept and celebrate those differences." —Audre Lorde

I learned a lot about thinking differently from building ducks. As part of a training session with

my consulting partners, we were each given six pieces of Lego. The pieces were "duck-coloured"—yellow and orange. One piece had an eye.

We were asked to build a duck. With only six pieces, it felt to me that there was only one clear way to build it. The trainer set the timer, and when it went off, we all showcased our creations. I was amazed to see that every one of the 10 people in the room created something different. Rather than (as it had initially seemed to me) one clear outcome, there were actually multiple alternatives.

The lesson for me was to broaden my lens. I began to recognize that my way of thinking was not *the* way of thinking, just as my truth wasn't *the* truth. I learned this lesson both at work and at home.

My husband and I are wired differently and much of our fighting occurs around how we make decisions. I am quick to make decisions and he needs time to process. In a recent case, I had decided that I wanted to plan a family vacation. I started some initial research and then suggested to my husband that we should go in May to Costa Rica. He had some questions. "Why May? It will be too hot." I said, "Okay, April," and scurried back to my computer to find flights and hotels that would work for that date. I came back with my "facts" and then he said, "I don't think we can afford it right now. Maybe we should wait until next year." I went back to my computer, ran the budget, looked at our cash flow, and came back to him with: "See, we can afford it if we just cut back on X, Y and Z." This was our typical decision-making process. I would come up with an idea and continue to present my facts until he conceded.

We have been married for 17 years. It was only in year 15 that I actually realized that this was not the best approach for either of us. I started to feel like he had "a problem for every solution" and he started to resent me for always pushing my ideas on him. I was not involving him in the process until I had all the "facts." I countered by saying that if I didn't come to him with the facts, then he would shut down the idea up front. This was our usual operating procedure. And then came Enneagram. This is a different type of assessment that gets at the underlying motivators or fears in how you operate. Each Enneagram type has a set of core beliefs that will motivate them to take particular actions and guide them to make certain decisions.

My husband Mike is a Loyal Skeptic (6) and I am an Enthusiastic Visionary (7). Loyal Skeptics are realists and like to consider all potential outcomes. They avoid risk. Enthusiastic Visionaries are optimists who seek joy at all costs, often not considering the implications of their choices. Here is a brief description of our motivations.

Type 6 The Loyalist	Committed, responsible, anxious and suspicious. Dislike unpredictability and rapid change, attracted to clear structures and foresight.
Type 7 The Enthusiast	Spontaneous, versatile, talkative and scattered. Dislike limitations and routines, attracted to new possibilities and excitement.

Source: Adapted from Brown, Anna & Bartram, Dave. (2005). Relationships between OPQ and Enneagram Types. SHL Group.

One of the big "a-ha" moments for me was when the colleague who ran the test explained the dynamic between him and his wife (also a 6 and 7). He asked me, "Isn't it great that every time you have a crazy idea, you have your husband to bring you back to reality?" My first instinct was to scream "NO. That drives me crazy. I have lots of ideas and he shuts down every one." But the more I reflected on it, the more I realized that I was the problem in this situation. I did not recognize his needs, his way of processing, his perspective. I did not appreciate the diversity he was offering me. I just wanted to have my way.

So Mike and I talked about it and learned more about how each other works and what we need. He needed to be involved up front and have time to consider all the potential scenarios. I needed to know that he was interested in my ideas and would support me with ways to achieve them. I also had to be willing to give up on my ideas if they didn't make sense. I had to recognize that his Lego duck was different.

Diversity of thought is essential in decision making. We are all influenced by our experience and teams must leverage this to their advantage. In 2015, McKinsey reviewed 366 public companies and evaluated their financial performance against the ethnic and racial diversity in their management team. Those with the most diversity were likely to have 35 percent better financial returns than the industry average. Research shows that diverse teams focus more on facts, process facts more carefully, and are more innovative. It is both profitable and ethical to engage with those who are different from us.

Leaders who bring people together to make decisions must make sure they build different ducks. They need to consider the people who are part of the conversation and ask three questions:

- Who's not here?
- Why aren't they here?
- What do I need to do to change that?

Truth Warriors create teams that bring different perspectives. They need to recognize that their duck is likely going to differ from someone else's. They understand the benefit of that. They need to bring in the right people to create diversity of thought. They need to broaden their lens and see that their truth is not *the* truth. They need to avoid pushing their perspectives and "YaBut" conversations.

"You can't read the label from inside the jar."
—Unknown

Avoid the YaBut.

I regularly turn to my sister for advice. Most recently I was asking her about whether I should allow my teenage son to put a TV in his room. She suggested that perhaps he is old enough to self-regulate. I responded with "Yes, but I'm not sure I trust him enough yet to make the best decisions." She then suggested that I put timeframes around his watching. "Yes, but how will I enforce it?" She told me about some apps that allow parents to track screen time. I responded with "Yes, but that feels too structured." I had worn her down. She said "It sounds like you don't want to allow him to put a TV in his room." I told her that was the case.

My sister is fond of reminding me that I am a pro at what she calls the "YaBut" conversation. When I ask for advice or feedback, I am almost always looking for validation. My goal is to get reassurance that my intuitive thoughts are right. So, I ask for "advice" and then when someone provides a counter-suggestion to my original belief, I say "Ya but…" and then reiterate and reinforce my opinion. At the end of the discussion, I feel very confident in my decision because I have addressed all the counterarguments. In reality, I haven't really listened to the alternatives. After one of these conversations has taken place, my sister will often ask, "Why did you ask for my advice?"

In business, YaBut's are looking to validate their decisions. They look for "YesMen." They surround themselves with people who agree with them. A "YesMan" is a person who does not express contrary points of view. They are perceived as suck-ups with their primary goal being to move up in the organization. But this may not always be the case. Oftentimes, they are working within a culture or with a leader who reinforces the view that dissent is bad. They may have also been shut down in trying to express an alternative perspective, as I did to my sister.

Leaders play a role in discouraging YesMen by avoiding the YaBut conversation. They need to approach conversations and decisions with a desire to explore and not to validate. One great way to do this is by starting broad instead of narrow. When looking for solutions to a defined problem, don't begin with your opinion but allow the group to hypothesize on the various alternatives. A great build to this is to allow the contribution to happen anonymously by asking team members to put their ideas on sticky notes or within a virtual discussion board. Assuming you allow for diverse perspectives, this should give you a good starting point for some alternatives to consider.

As the group starts to work towards a solution, you may start to feel yourself disagreeing. Pause and ask yourself why. This is a great opportunity to WAIT—to ask yourself, "Why am I talking?" Instead, use this as your opportunity to listen and understand. It is the most difficult part of the conversation for me. It is a time when I have to stop myself from selling my ideas and instead open my mind to other possibilities.

Leaders tend to be strong visionaries. They see a future and patterns that others may not. It is tempting when you feel like the group is going in the wrong direction to redirect. You may be correct in thinking their ideas won't work, but you want to be sure. This is your opportunity to avoid the "YaBut." When the group is going against the direction you think they should, ask them to help you understand their perspective better.

Letting go of your opinion will strengthen the result. One CEO shared this thought: "If you go in with an idea, or a thought, or if you're predisposed to some decision and you come out and it looks different, you've probably come out better for it." You have allowed the opportunity to consider alternatives. In addition, by engaging the team in discussion, you've enabled people to really understand why and how the decision will be made.

Truth Warriors encourage their teams to challenge them and each other. They are open in their desire for alternatives, even if it seems counterintuitive to what they believe is the right solution. They ask questions and avoid the temptation to validate their existing thinking. They support honest, direct feedback and know that they need to be kind, not nice.

"If you are irritated by every rub, how will you be polished?" —*Rumi*

Be kind, not nice.

Back in the corporate world, I was put on an "acceleration team." Our goal was to take some off-the-wall ideas and pressure-test them to see if they were worth investing in. The team had representation across all functional areas. We were probably more likeminded than we should have been but we had been assembled as thought leaders within the company to try to co-create something new. Linda was our representative from marketing and assigned as the lead for our team. She was brilliant and had a lot of new ideas. I enjoyed bantering with her as part of the process. Linda was also very disorganized. Although she was collaborative when we were together, she would often forget to send us important information that was coming through to her that would inform our decisions. She would schedule last-minute meetings. I was getting frustrated working with her and was hearing similar grumblings from others on the team. Initially, we were complaining to one another. What started as an offhanded comment like "Linda forgot again" started to become a logging of complaints. Side conversations happened and many began to question whether Linda was capable of leading. We were in the process of triangulation. Triangulation is a process that happens far too often in teams. It is the process whereby one person is frustrated with someone but rather than communicate directly with that person, they talk to a third person. It is the polite way of saying they are "talking behind someone's back."

Miguel was the Finance representative on our team. He had only been with the company about three months. He didn't know anyone on the team until we began working together. He happened to walk into one of our complaint sessions. Three of us were waiting for the meeting to start and we were complaining about how Linda had called yet another last-minute meeting. When Miguel walked in, he heard me say, "She doesn't seem to care about us at all. She has no respect for our time." Miguel sat down and joined the group. He started by saying he understood our frustration but then asked, "Who has spoken to Linda about this?" We looked sheepishly back at him. We had a lot of respect for Linda. We knew she was trying hard to get this right and even though what she was doing was irritating, we didn't want to hurt her feelings. Miguel said, "Sometimes to be kind, you can't be nice. Linda may not know the impact she is having on us. She will lead other teams, and if we don't tell her about our frustrations, it may affect her overall performance later. We need to tell her." Miguel was right, and I did as he suggested.

It was an uncomfortable conversation. I knew my intentions were good, and thankfully Linda and I had built up enough trust that she listened openly to my feedback. She was apologetic. It was difficult for her to hear that she was causing frustrations on the team. I tried to assure her that she offered great value and that we just needed her to adjust some of her behaviours. She committed to working at it. Her willingness to listen and Miguel's advice had a major impact on the team. She only had to make minor shifts—planning ahead for meetings and being careful to quickly share everything that came across her desk that would be relevant—but the difference was huge. The team recognized her effort, forgave her if she didn't get it right, and felt more confident in sharing feedback with one another.

This was one of many difficult feedback conversations I have had in my career. It's fair to say that I probably didn't get it totally right. I have subsequently learned a better way. I use a variation of the SBI model created by the Center for Creative Leadership, with two further additions. It is called ISBIQ: Intentions, Situation, Behaviour, Impact, Questions.

It starts with positive intent. My intentions with Linda were to strengthen the team and set her up for future success. If you are providing feedback, it is important to start by stating your Intention—saying why you are doing so and demonstrating that you genuinely care about them. The next step is to discuss the Situation: it is the context for why you are providing the feedback. It should provide a specific event tied to the undesired behaviour. The Behaviour component should outline the specific observable behaviours. This is where you need to be very careful not to offer judgements or inferences. I would have gone wrong with Linda if I had said "you weren't very considerate of our time." Instead, I needed to focus on what she did. This moves us into the Impact or the implications of the behaviours. The Questions portion of the feedback should allow for interaction. Feedback should not be one way. It is important to understand the other person's reaction and engage them in the solution. From that perspective, my Linda conversation should have sounded something like this:

INTENT: "Linda, I wanted to talk to you about something that I think will strengthen the team."
SITUATION: "In our last few meetings…"
BEHAVIOURS: "…you have booked time for us to meet on the same day."
IMPACT: "As a result, the team needs to scramble to make time for the meeting and are not as prepared as they would like to be."
QUESTION: "How do you think we can avoid this scramble in the future?

Telling an employee they are not performing is one of the hardest conversations leaders have. The only conversation harder would be the one telling an employee they are being let go. Both of these conversations require a willingness to make a difficult decision and to lean in to conflict. You need to be able to decide how to handle what appears to be poor performance. You need to decide whose fault it is. (Hint: it is likely the fault of both of you.) You need to align on and communicate how to fix the problem. You need to provide direct, honest feedback. All of these things are very challenging, especially for new leaders.

I have known many managers who have kept people in jobs or roles way too long. The person was not performing and because the manager was not able to first identify the issue and second (and most importantly) *discuss* the issue, the issue was not fully resolved. This situation is usually not good for anyone. The manager is frustrated, the employee likely feels they aren't doing their best work, and the organization suffers.

Leaders have the opportunity to build a culture of radical transparency. We have an inherent desire for harmony. Oftentimes our excuse when we avoid difficult conversations is our desire to be nice. Instead, it is kinder to be forthright in our feedback and in the conversations we need to hold in order to make better decisions. Sometimes you need to fight the battle (respectfully) to avoid the war.

Truth Warriors engage in difficult conversations. They avoid sidebar conversations and speak directly and respectfully to their teams and others. They do so to support greatness. They know that it is kinder to be forthright in your feedback than to refrain from saying what is uncomfortable just to spare someone's feelings. They are humble and bold.

26. Be Humble and Bold

*"Judging a person does not define who they are.
It defines who you are." —Unknown*

Put down the pitchfork.

On Thursday, June 14, 2019 the Toronto Raptors made history by being the first Canadian team to win the NBA title. It was a proud day for Canadians: 44 percent of Canada's population (15.9 million people) tuned in to watch some part of the game. I was one of them. It was the first basketball game I had watched that year. I am not a huge sports fan but I do like to support my local teams, particularly when they are playing an important game. I also fiercely celebrated the win by the Toronto Blue Jays in 1992. I am a self-admitted bandwagon-jumper.

Bandwagon jumping is an idiom that describes the act of joining others or changing your opinion to support something that is likely to be successful. It supports our desire to win. (In my defense, I also support the Toronto Maple Leafs who have a long history of losing.) It is not uncommon for people to be moved by the momentum of others' success. Nor is it problematic, unless the bandwagon is going in the wrong direction or turns in to a witch hunt by an angry mob.

Too many times, fueled by social media, people jump on a bandwagon of inaccurate information without consideration for the context or perspective of the person they may be persecuting. Ellen DeGeneres is a recent example of this tendency. She has been a successful talk show host since 2003. In 2020, amidst the pandemic, news started to circulate that maybe she wasn't as nice as she appeared to be. With very little concrete evidence, fans started to turn on her. The bandwagon left the barn, and people were happy to pile on the hate. I personally can't say if she is guilty of some of the accusations. From afar, it appears her army did not act in the way she expected and the result was a toxic work environment. As a leader, she has a role to play in that. At the same time, should that negate the last 17 years she spent helping people? The reality is that no one is in a position to judge her. I read a story by Jonathan Kestenbaum that demonstrates how our perspective impacts our judgement:

> A young couple moved into a new neighbourhood. The next morning while they were eating breakfast, the young woman saw her neighbour hanging the washing outside. "That laundry is not very clean; she doesn't know how to wash correctly. Perhaps she needs better laundry soap." Her husband looked on, remaining silent. Every time her neighbour hung her washing out to dry, the young woman made the same comments. A month later, the woman was surprised to see a nice clean wash on the line and said to her husband, "Look, she's finally learned how to wash correctly. I wonder who taught her this?" The husband replied, "I got up early this morning and cleaned our windows."

We see the world through our own distorted lens. What we see may be a result of our own misperceptions or bias. In decision-making, our judgement of others closes our minds. If you already believe that their ideas are crazy or their beliefs are wrong, you will struggle to open your mind to alternatives. Letting go of judgment is a challenge for me. My daughter taught me a valuable lesson in this regard.

She was about 5 years old at the time. She was making a craft and asked me to cut her out a heart from construction paper. I was working but paused to do what she asked. She said, "It's not big enough." I asked her to bring me a new piece of paper and then I cut her a bigger heart. She went away to begin her craft and returned a few minutes later saying that she messed it up and could I please cut her another one. I was getting frustrated with her ongoing requests. I told her that I didn't have the time to do it right then and it was going to have to be good enough. She walked away disappointed. She returned a short while later. I was about ready to erupt when she said, "Mommy, this card is for you. I wanted it to be perfect like you but I know you didn't have the time to help me fix it. I hope it is okay." She had written "Mom" on the heart and had run out of room. She had tried to squeeze the last "M" on. I had judged her harshly and was frustrated by her needs, instead of embracing what she was trying to achieve.

Truth Warriors keep an open mind and avoid jumping on the wrong bandwagon. They put their pitchforks down when an angry mob persecutes someone with very little information. Instead they try to suspend judgement and replace it with curiosity and interest. They try to understand the perspectives of others. They lead with humility.

> **Eat the pie, but not the meat.**

"At the risk of sounding immodest, I have no flaws. Unless of course you find me immodest, and then I do in fact have one flaw."
—Alex P. Keaton (*Family Ties*)

In July 2008, public health units in Ontario noticed a sudden spike in cases of listeriosis. Listeriosis is an intestinal infection which is spread by ingesting contaminated foods such as ready-to-eat meats, soft cheeses, milk and raw vegetables. Upon investigation, they traced the outbreak back to a Toronto manufacturing plant making deli meat for Maple Leaf Foods. Michael McCain was the CEO at the time.

McCain acted quickly. Before the link was fully traced to their plant, McCain had already issued a voluntary recall. Once confirmed, he issued a further recall to include multiple facilities. More importantly, he took personal responsibility. In a press conference he said, "Knowing there is a desire to assign blame, the buck stops here. I emphasize: this is our accountability and it's ours to fix." He also apologized directly to the Canadian public through a commercial in which he declared "our best efforts failed and we are deeply sorry." Michael McCain was brave and humble in his declaration.

The dictionary defines being humble as "having a modest opinion or estimate of one's own importance, rank, etc." As McCain did, it takes humility to recognize and own up to one's own weakness.

The world is filled with great leaders who demonstrate humility. Leaders who put themselves in the trenches with their people instead of directing from above. Canadian prime minister Justin Trudeau personally welcomed Syrian refugees at the airport with winter coats. Dutch prime minister Mark Rutte mopped up coffee spilled by him while walking into the Ministry of Health. Jacinda Ardern, the prime minister of New Zealand, wore a modest headscarf and visited the neighbourhoods impacted by the terrorist attack on a mosque in Christchurch. She attended the memorial services and spoke minimally, preferring instead to allow more time for the families to share their grief.

Barack Obama is a leader known for his humility. I was privileged to see him speak in early 2020 at a conference held by the Economic Council of Canada. It was a Q&A session and one of the last questions he was asked was a strange one. The interviewer asked him that if he could choose to be any woman in the world, who he would be. Frankly, I anticipated that he might answer with something around the lines of Oprah Winfrey or Ellen DeGeneres. Instead, he said that he would choose to be a mother in a developing country. He said that he wanted everyone to "put yourself in the eyes of a mother who is powerless to help their child."

Each leader I spoke to in writing this book, whether they were rational or intuitive, conflict assertive or adverse, talked to me about humility. Each stressed the importance of recognizing the need to make clear that they do not have all the answers and are as capable of making mistakes as anyone else on their team. One leader I spoke to offered a powerful example of humility in leadership:

> If you don't have the right culture, you can't have the right decision-making because good decision-making means people are going to be right, wrong, and open and vulnerable and insulted and angry and you have to be able to reconcile all of that in a safe manner. How I deal with it is that I try to expose that I'm not perfect and others are valuable in what they say. That allows me to challenge openly without my authority biasing the process. I'm the founder and I'm the president and CEO and really all final decisions stop with

me but I can be a detriment to the process, because if people view my authority as absolute, then they won't offer their best ideas up. I always say that we are all equals in this. None of us are more or worse. I have the ability to really delve deep into something and people know that so people may not want to offer their advice because they think that I might already know the answer and that's not true at all. I have ideas and knowledge, but I have really big blind spots or ignorance or other things that I don't know and I am really interested in their opinion. So in order to make a decision, you need to empower the people that have the knowledge to be able to offer the knowledge but also make sure that they feel safe enough that they can realize when their opinion, although it's good, might need to bend a little bit to meet the other aspects of the company.

Truth Warriors know the benefits of eating humble pie and acknowledging mistakes and weakness. They don't claim to be the smartest person in the room or need to have all the answers. They recognize their blind spots and look for diverse perspectives to supplement their knowledge. They see the light in others but also sometimes need to follow the darkness.

> "Fear is a reaction. Courage is a decision."
> —*Winston Churchill*

Follow the darkness.

When I was young, we had a basement with a cold cellar in it. Inevitably, my mom would ask me to go down and get something out of there. It felt like a long, dimly lit walk and I always sped in and out as quickly as I could. Even as I became an adult, my fear of that long walk didn't change. Rationally, I knew there was nothing in there. But fear of the unknown is a powerful thing.

One week after 9/11, a Gallup poll asked the U.S. public if they were worried about a family member being a victim of terrorism. Fifty-one percent of respondents said they were. This in itself is not surprising: 3008 people died as a result of that incident. What is surprising is that 15 years later that percentage was still the same, despite the fact that deaths as a result of terrorism for the total of those 15 subsequent years is 207. Fear makes us hold onto beliefs that are irrational. It stops us from moving forward.

We have a friend of the family we visit every once in a while. Although I love her, and our visits are pleasant enough, I always leave feeling frustrated. She is in her mid-seventies and at each visit reminds me of the things she wishes she could do. She has been expressing these same sentiments for the past 20 years. She has always wanted to go to Hawaii. Her husband doesn't want to go with her. I ask her why she doesn't ask a friend to go. (She has plenty.) She finds some excuse. What holds her back is her inability to take action, and yet she feels remorse. She doesn't recognize her own ability to change her life.

I see this all the time with my clients and even some of my friends. They want a different career or to follow a new path. But they don't act on that desire. They don't believe that they can. They are paralyzed by indecision or their inability to ask for help. They don't know which path to take, so they don't take any. Fear can be expressed in terms of two different acronyms: Forget Everything and Run, or Face Everything and Rise.

Nothing frustrates me more than someone who misses out on their dreams because they are afraid to pursue them. I struggle even more so if I can see the path forward, and they cannot. Growing up, I had a friend who suffered from depression. It was the 1980s and mental health was not really a thing. I'm not even sure my teenage self understood that she was suffering. What I saw was someone who felt hopeless. Any attempt for me to cheer her up or suggest alternatives to her unhappiness were met with "that will never work" or "nothing will ever change." It was infuriating for me. I felt helpless. I know a lot more about depression now than I did then but admittedly I still struggle with those who are unwilling to see another way. For me it's like watching someone drown when I have a life raft that they refuse to take.

I have also learned to recognize that sometimes it is me that is drowning. I am the one who doesn't see the raft that is being offered. Sometimes when we are overwhelmed, we forgot to look for the light. We forget the dreams we are chasing, or the long-term benefits of doing what is uncomfortable. It is easy to get lost in darkness. It's even easier to try and avoid it altogether.

In business, when leaders avoid the darkness, they cannot move forward. Risk is always a part of growth and leaders need to be willing to venture in to the unknown. Being comfortable with being uncomfortable is an important part of that. Recognizing that no decision will please everyone is essential. It means letting go of the belief that "if I try, I might fail." It also means being willing to face rejection. In his TED Talk, "What I Learned from 100 Days of Rejection," Jia Jiang offers an inspiring view of how we can not only reduce the pain of rejection, but thrive as a result of rejection.

Jia Jiang was initially inspired by a game introduced by a Canadian entrepreneur named Jason Comely. He had a website called "Rejection Therapy." The game forced you to find ways to be rejected for 30 days. Jia took this to a new level and instead aimed for 100 days. His journey started with fear and embarrassment but ended with some amazing lessons. He learned that if he was brave enough to persist rather than walk away when he got rejected, he could sometimes turn a "no" into a "yes." Anticipating rejection, Jia asked a random stranger if he could plant flowers in his backyard. The man said "No" and when Jia asked "Why?" he explained that he had a dog and it would be a waste of the flowers, but that he had a neighbour who loved flowers. Jia planted his flowers in her backyard. He had gotten a referral. He was successful because he took the time to understand why he was being rejected instead of making assumptions. Like all great leaders, he also recognized the benefit of humility. By openly acknowledging the strangeness of his request and showing vulnerability, he was able to convince a Starbucks manager to let him be a "Starbucks greeter" (similar to a Walmart greeter but at Starbucks). Jia Jiang has made a career of getting rejected. He now owns the website "Rejection Therapy" and helps others to thrive in the face of rejection.

One of my favourite songs is "Brave" by Sara Bareilles. I actually use it as my ring tone. If you watch the video, you will see a group of people dancing (reasonably well) in public. The video appears to be filmed without the initial knowledge of the onlookers. The dancers are willing to look silly or stand out against the crowd. There are a few instances in the video where the dancers ask others to join them. At a bus stop, one man reaches out and asks someone to join him and is ignored by everyone. He continues to dance. Others have more success and are able to convince people to dance with them. Even those who weren't as willing to dance enjoyed the show. Most of the time we celebrate others who are brave and yet when we consider being brave ourselves, we fear rejection. The key is to take it less personally and enjoy the dance.

Truth Warriors still fear the darkness. Fear is inevitable. They recognize the fear in themselves and they look down that dark staircase and run for that can of peas, no matter how scary it is. They know that bravery is fear in motion. They embrace rejection and take the path less travelled. They are comfortable being uncomfortable. They take risks and they know the best way to be successful is to take more shots.

Take more shots.

"You miss 100 percent of the shots you don't take." —*Wayne Gretzky*

My son, who has anxiety, plays hockey. For him, the sport is both a constant source of fun and fear. In particular, he becomes stressed before games. He is worried that he will fail. When he plays, he is often reluctant to shoot on the net, although he is an excellent passer. Last year, he had the most assists of anyone on the team. Although I did celebrate the fact that he supported the team rather than focusing on individual achievement, I suspected that was not his main motivation. When I asked him about it, he told me that he was afraid that if he shot and missed, he would fail. I reminded him of Wayne Gretzky's message by telling him, "You'll miss every shot if you don't try." Truly a perfect quotation for most situations but especially this one. And at the next game, he took a shot—and the goalie stopped it. Every next shot, he passed (another assist). When he got off the ice he said to me, "See, Mom, I shot and I didn't score."

Unfortunately, this analogy is true for many of us. We allow ourselves to take the risk and then fail only to justify our belief that we shouldn't have taken the risk to begin with. But, of course, in my hockey analogy, the *more* you shoot, the more likely you are to score. There is a huge correlation between risk and reward.

Leaning in to conflict is all about being willing to take that risk. To recognize the reward instead of the potential failure in having that difficult conversation. And like every good hockey player, you can sharpen your skills before you take the shot. You are going to miss more shots if you never practice. You need to practice conflict and risk-taking. You need to get good at it. You need to equip yourself with the tools to be successful.

Taking risks starts with having confidence in yourself and the decisions you are making. There are both simple and in-depth tools to analyze risk. A question we often use with our son when we feel his anxiety rising is: "Is this a mountain or a molehill?" It helps him to put in perspective the level of his problem. When the fear is bubbling up, it encourages him to think about the impact.

Leaders can ask the same questions of themselves and their teams. What are the implications if we get this wrong? How will this affect our team, the organization? Will this cause severe emotional distress? Will it be easy to course-correct if we get this wrong?

A more advanced way is to compare the potential consequences or impact against the probability of the risk occurring in a matrix such as the one to the right.

If we take the time up front to under-

Impact	Probability 1	Probability 2	Probability 3
3	Significant Risk	Major Risk	Maximum Risk
2	Minor Risk	Significant Risk	Major Risk
1	Minor Risk	Minor Risk	Significant Risk

stand the risk, we're more likely to make better decisions that prevent it. Even if it is not preventable, having identified it should require further thought in to how to address it, if the risk occurs.

Truth Warriors take risks. They take more shots, knowing that one failure does not stop them from winning the game. They balance their fear of failure with a calculated understanding of how to avoid it. They are cautious but also courageous, and they recognize brave in others.

Recognize brave in others.

"I've learned so much from my mistakes, I think I'll go make some more." —Cheryl Cole

Nancy was a VP of sales at a pharmaceutical company we worked with. Her goal was to create more accountability in her team. She felt that her people were timid and unwilling to share their ideas. She wanted them to be able to have the crucial conversations she felt were necessary to drive innovation. Her team was relatively new, so we built out a program that started with building trust. We facilitated an exercise to allow them to articulate and capture a common vision for the team. One of the first things I noticed is that whenever one of her team members offered a unique solution, Nancy challenged it. She asked them why they thought that way and if it made sense when set against the corporate vision. Some of the team members continued to express their perspectives, but many did not.

When I debriefed with Nancy after, she said, "You see what I mean? They are afraid to speak up." Nancy valued direct feedback. She wanted her team to 'fight for their ideas" but she did not recognize that when they did, they were being dismissed. I asked Nancy to think about her role in the meeting. Was there anything she might have done differently? Did she think everyone felt heard? With further coaching, Nancy was able to see that as the leader, she needed to acknowledge and recognize when her team needed the space to be brave.

Greg Smith's book *In Search of Safe Brave Spaces* is a great resource for leaders looking develop these spaces within organizations and within themselves. It starts with understanding yourself and your triggers, and offers strategies to create intentional dialogue between communities. One idea Greg presents but doesn't necessarily advocate is called the "IDEAS Cage Match." In partnership with TED, Autodesk set up a mock fight that would pit one idea against another. Big ideas like "Evolution vs. Interference" and "Abundance vs. Scarcity." It is a process to release healthy debate with the aim of advancing an idea. It is a fun, safe way to hear both sides of the story.

Leaders have the ability to facilitate similar dialogue—without the gloves or cage. They need to encourage both sides of an argument and reward employees for participating, speaking their minds, and respecting different opinions.

Recognizing brave also requires that leaders allow for mistakes and reward risk-taking. Great companies recognize the need to celebrate failure as part of their culture. Huntsman Corporation, a chemical manufacturer, offers an example of this culture. A contractor was responsible for installing scaffolding on their site. In doing so, he made a mistake which caused chemicals to leak into the river. He informed the company promptly and when his contracting company heard about the mistake they fired him. However, hearing this news, Huntsman insisted he be reinstated and threw a party to celebrate. They recognized that because the contractor confessed to his mistake immediately the leak was fixed in 30 minutes instead of the chemical pouring in to the river for the next 24 hours. The contractor owned his mistake, improved the situation and was rewarded.

There are many great examples of companies who recognize brave in others and celebrate failure. Intuit, an accounting software company, holds "failure parties" to celebrate what has been learned from their mistakes. The Indian multinational Tata Group created a prize for "best failed idea."

One leader I spoke to shared her approach to recognizing and supporting brave. She uses authenticity circles: 20 minutes at each team meeting for each person to share something that isn't work related. It allowed people the opportunity to be vulnerable and get to know each other in a more personal way. It was key that she was also a role model in her willingness to share.

Truth Warriors understand that failure is essential to learning. They encourage bravery and reward employees when they have difficult conversations with them and with others. They understand the need to role model this behaviour themselves: to be vulnerable and open to perspectives from their teams. They know that sometimes you need to rock the boat.

Rock the boat.

"I prefer people who rock the boat to people who jump out." —*Orson Welles*

In the midst of one of the largest racial conflicts in my history, I was inspired by the image below and the message it represents. It is a picture of the medal ceremony for the men's 200-metre race at the 1968 Olympics. The two Black men with their arms raised are U.S. athletes Tommie Smith and John Carlos. Peter Norman, an Australian sprinter, won silver. All three are wearing OPHR (Olympic Project for Human Rights) badges. The founder of the organization actually encouraged Black athletes to boycott the Games.

The two Black men removed their shoes for the ceremony and were wearing black socks. They did so as a representation of Black poverty. The gloves and fists raised were a symbol of Black oppression. The beads around their necks were to protest lynchings of Black people in the southern U.S. As a result of their protest, both men were banned from the Olympics and returned home to condemnation and death threats to their families.

An image of this event was presented to me as part of a leadership

ANGELO COZZI (MONDADORI PUBLISHERS)

roundtable in July 2020 by Wes Hall, the founder of the Black-North Initiative. He shared their story with us, but more surprising was this statement: "Peter Norman was actually the person who sacrificed the most."

Peter Norman was a believer in the rights of Blacks, but at the time Australia had not yet completely dismantled restrictions on non-white immigration and was also mistreating Australian Aboriginals. He asked his fellow medalists what he could do to support them. They asked him to wear the OPHR badge as a sign of support. As a result of this action, he was ostracized upon his return. Despite having qualified 13 times over, he was not chosen for the 1972 Australian Olympic team. Norman did not go on to lead the life he deserved. He turned to alcohol and drugs and died at the age of 64 in 2006. Smith and Carlos were pallbearers at his funeral.

Peter Norman never ran in the Olympics again, but he kept his silver medal. In the 2008 documentary *Salute*, Norman himself said of his actions: "There was a social injustice that I couldn't do anything about from where I was, but I certainly hated it. It has been said that sharing my silver medal with that incident on the victory detracted from my performance. On the contrary. I have to confess I was rather proud to be part of it." It was not until after his death that the Australian government acknowledged its mistake in restricting his career and the sacrifice he made for human rights.

Peter Norman made a huge personal sacrifice for what he believed in. I also have seen companies risk profits for a greater cause. In May 2020, Twitter was the first of the social media giants to take a stand against misinformation by labeling tweets from President Trump as potentially misleading. They encouraged their readers to "get the facts." Shortly after that, they put a warning on a tweet in which the president threatened violence to protesters, declaring "when the looting starts, the shooting starts." The president responded with an executive order that would prevent any social media company from restricting free speech. He also called Twitter's head of site integrity, Yoel Roth, a "hater" and his staff encouraged the public to harass him.

Jack Dorsey, the CEO of Twitter, responded as every leader should, taking responsibility for his decision and asking people to stay away from Roth. He tweeted out, "There is someone ultimately accountable for our actions as a company, and that's me." Jack Dorsey took on a giant with a large following among the American public. He did it to combat misinformation and hate.

In 2015, Target took a bold step in removing gender-based signs in their toy sections. The move was in reaction to a parent who posted a picture of signs labelled "building sets" and "girls' building sets." Although Target received praise for the move, there was also harsh criticism and calls to boycott the retailer. Target is not a stranger to pushing a broader agenda. In the 1960s, it began to use black models in its advertising, a practice that was very limited at the time. In 2016, it continued to advance human rights by declaring that transgender individuals were welcome to use the restrooms that corresponded to their gender identity. Again the company faced backlash.

Companies that make bold, controversial decisions are backed by brave leaders. Brian Cornell, the CEO of Target, was the leader who supported the removal of the gender-based signs and allowed transgender people to choose the appropriate restroom. In May 2020, in response to the death of George Floyd, he addressed his team and community with an open letter that ended in the following statement: "Since we opened our doors, Target has operated with love and opportunity for all. And in that spirit, we commit to contributing to a city and community that will turn the pain we're all experiencing into better days for everyone."

Truth Warriors are willing to rock the boat when the boat needs rocking. They are bold in their choices, even in the face of challenging consequences. They stand up for what they believe and what is right. They push against the status quo. They seek truth, they speak truth and they lead truth.

Conclusion

The battle of the Truth Warrior is not easy. The dance can sometimes feel impossible. It is finding the balance. It is recognizing the need to move, within ourselves and with one another. It starts with knowing who you are and who you want to become. It embraces failure. It challenges you to think differently.

The Truth Warrior must be a Scout and a Soldier. You must seek truth with a balance of systematic logic and gut instinct. You must rely on others and build systems to challenge your own beliefs. You must trust a little and trust a lot.

The Truth Warrior understands the benefit of silence and yet knows the importance of sharing their voice. The world needs your ideas. The world needs your voice. You need to share it and you need to encourage others to do the same.

The Truth Warrior is a leader. You are brave and bold. You are humble and respectful. You understand the importance of tension and diversity of thought. No matter how you naturally make decisions or embrace conflict, you move within truth.

The path ahead is not easy. It is yours to take. You can arm yourself with the right tools. You will sometimes fail. But like every Warrior before you, you will continue on. Sometimes the dance you do will be one of victory. The Truth Warrior is within you. The battle is before you. Your journey awaits.

Additional Resources

Throughout this book you will have seen this icon in the margins of various pages. It indicates that additional resources are available to you: videos, downloadable tools or links to other useful content. You can find all these resources at:

www.truthwarriors.ca/resources

Acknowledgements

This book would not be possible without the army of Truth Warriors who inspire me and my tribe of Truth Warriors who help me in my battle.

I want to start at the beginning by thanking Sarah McVanel-Viney for challenging me to write the book I didn't know I needed to write and all of my fellow authors at the GreatnessBizBook Writing Intensive who helped me through the ups and down of crafting my story.

To my partners at Lighthouse NINE who lift me up every day and have helped me to shape my business and the lessons that I share in this book. Thank you Phil, Marnie, Cindy, Drew, Gemma, Greg, Dave, Warren, Kim, Nancy, Corinne and Sheena.

To the leaders I interviewed who shared their battle scars with me: Luc Mongeau, Lee Ferreira, Tara Greenwood, Phil Drouillard, Drew Munro and Bruce and Jenn Tunnicliffe.

To my early readers who helped shape my message and nudged me along when the I got lost in the darkness: Brea, Leanne, Phil, Drew, Greg, Jenn, Jodi and Marg.

To Michele Ireland for her legal advice and ongoing guidance.

To Liane Davey for her mentorship as I navigated this new world.

To Azadeh Yaraghi for helping to shape the look and feel of the branding for the book.

To Alan Yearwood, my audiobook producer at Thinking Audio for listening to every word multiple times and reminding me of the impact my words can have.

To The Garden North America Inc. and the work of Dic Dickerson and Adriana Mahalean, to whose brilliance I owe the beautiful cover design.

To my publisher, David Stover at Rock's Mills Press, for taking a chance on me and taking me under his wing so that I could become an author.

To my book club who provided guidance along the way and have agreed to include this book on the docket; Nicole, Michele, Karen, Cheryl, and Kathy.

To those leaders who helped me validate my messaging; Denise, Scott, Emily, Maude, Ryan, Rojzen, Laurel, and Michelle M.

To all my friends who have listened to the ups and downs of my journey and continue to challenge me to think differently.

To my sister, who has battled beside me and against me from the first day she was born. She is the yin to my yang and can always be counted on to call me out on my "yabuts."

To my dad who always believed in me and taught me the importance of understanding others. To my stepmother Angie, for supporting him in his journey and for her ongoing role in our lives.

To my mom who was my first warrior. She taught me to be bold. She fought her battles so that I could be successful in fighting mine.

To my children, Alex, Aiden and Lauren. You are the most important part of my story. You are the future Truth Warriors and I am thankful for the lessons you have taught me.

To my husband Mike for loving me as we fight our battles together. Thank you for reminding me that everyone builds different ducks, that my truth is not THE truth and that there is beauty in our differences. Thank you for being part of my journey.

About the Author

Christi Scarrow has been helping individuals, teams and organizations to make decisions for more than twenty years. She is a consultant, trainer, speaker and executive coach. As a Partner at Lighthouse NINE Group, she works with multinational clients and small businesses across many diverse industries. Christi is an expert at finding clarity within uncertainty and simplicity from the complex. She helps leaders to be confident in the choices they make. She is passionate about building a world based on truth. She lives in the Greater Toronto Area with her husband and three children.

Made in the USA
Middletown, DE
20 May 2021

40146318R00106